Memories and Musings

Memories and Musings

Frances H. Kunzweiler

iUniverse, Inc.

New York Lincoln Shanghai

Memories and Musings

iUniverse books may be ordered through booksellers or by contacting:

iUniverse
2021 Pine Lake Road, Suite 100
Lincoln, NE 68512
www.iuniverse.com
1-800-Authors (1-800-288-4677)

Because of the dynamic nature of the Internet, any Web addresses or links contained in this book may have changed since publication and may no longer be valid.

ISBN: 978-0-595-46780-8 (pbk)
ISBN: 978-0-595-71373-8 (cloth)
ISBN: 978-0-595-91072-4 (ebk)

Printed in the United States of America

Contents

FOREWORD

This second book reveals some of my most inner thoughts, dreams, hopes and realities of my 93 years. Foremost is my strong faith and belief in God as evinced in many of my musings.

Blessed with longevity and good health, a great number of my life's observations and experiences are captured within these pages. The road is not always a smooth one, but traversed in the right spirit, joy follows sadness, daylight follows darkness, sunshine after rain, and as little Annie sang, "The Sun Will Come Up Tomorrow."

There is something for everyone, young and old. Topics about love, life, people, pets, history, nature, our nation, and more. Some things may tug at your memory, the ABCs. state capitals, our English language with multiple spellings and meanings of the same word. Enjoy!

I dedicate this book to my late husband, Joe, my son Don, my daughter Rita and my grandchildren Karen, Rick, Tim, Denny and Tricia; to their children Chelsea, Callahan, Joe, Stephanie; and my great-great grandchildren, Chase and Maddison. Each is in one way or another an inspiration.

Also I want to acknowledge Father Richard E. Grasso, and Father John J. O'Malley O.P., beloved priests and friends for their prayers and encouragement.

Finally to those who read this book, my family, friends, and good neighbors, thank you and May the Good Lord Bless and Keep You.

Deo Gratias,

Frances Helen Kunzweiler

MEMORIES

Attending St. Brendan's Catholic Church
September eleven twenty-0-four
Our prayers were for the many
Lives lost three years before.

My tears with many others
Hearts were filled with pain
Coming home we ask ourselves
What to do, help them to live again.

The wind is a mighty force
Traveling many miles
Trees broken like match sticks
Loss of power, phones and water
Wiping away many smiles.

'Canes boil on our ocean
And reach from shore to shore
Islands in the great Atlantic
Cause suffering to the poor.

I know there is a God
Pray all will do what's best
Realize He is the master
He puts us to the test.

STORM — 9/13/04

Hurricanes are on the way
Too blast the Florida state
We pray no lives are lost
Though damage will be great.

People being warned to leave
Will travel many miles
Endless hours trying to find
Gas, food and places to unwind.

Each state has their problems
North, south, east or west
Hurricane season lasts four months
Putting southern states to the test.

Without power, phones, conveniences
Only cell phones to communicate
Utility workers travel many miles
Thank you all angels in disguise
In God's heart you are great.

PATIENCE

Grant us forgiveness every day
Wisdom to understand
Why the world is topsy-turvy
In this our wonderland.

Opportunities are offered
Many creations to claim
Joy of understanding
Why seek a life of fame.

Human nature gives us courage
Why do some try to impress
Waste of time to dilly-dally
Look for incredible reasons for success.

Patience is a virtue
Has been for ages past
Fill your heart with caring, loving
Those memories long will last.

ATHENS

Names in the news everywhere
About Olympics of 2004
Youth from nations worldwide
Seeking for gold a perfect score.

A great country Greece, the host
Went back a thousand years
Worldwide newspapers and television
Give praise, applause, showing tears.

Athens though the ancient city
Host to hundreds of girls and boys
Also a name I treasure for relatives
Living in Athens, Illinois.

To the entrants of all countries
Be blessed in every way
If you took home a medal
Share with all each and everyday.

The Americans love their country
Just like all others do
The losers might win next time
Their names among "who's who".

THANK YOU

Thank you each and everyone
No matter age feel life just begun
Thanks for times of fun and laughter
Storing memories for long after.

The sun sinks in the west
Moon, stars do their best
Thanks for each day we live
Seek ways to forget and forgive.

Thinking took me back to yesteryear
As children seems we felt no fear
Thank you for days long past
For memories long will last.

Thank you Don, Rita, Karen too
May your lives long endure
Karen a granddaughter tried and true
Life passes quickly in review.

RAINBOW

The rainbow a work of art
After storm and rain
An arch of pastel colors
God's masterpiece will remain.

For each to make a wish
May they be ever bold
Say how far they might travel
To find a pot of gold.

We view waves from the ocean
Trees wafting by the wind
Smell fragrances from the flowers
Watch children as they swim.

Strength for us, love of life
Learning to forget, forgive
Each use power of imagination
Like water running through a sieve.

GOOD DEED

We like to feel someone will care
As we strive doing our share
Others standing idly by
Will they aid stop and try
Lend a hand, say a prayer
Ease a mind
Of someone in despair
We are taught one and all
In distress, place a call
Having found this isn't so
People stop and look
Then on they go
Acting in a hurry
Their thought
Why should I worry.
To always lend a hand
Some day you might need
Help from someone
Doing a good deed.

SNOW

Did you ever watch the snowflakes
Falling all around
Covering the earth white
Creating a quiet sound.

I waited for our newsboy
Come trudging down the street
Wishing if it keeps snowing
A no school day would be a treat.

Soon the sun was shining,
Trees and shrubbery seemed to nod their head
Glistening snowflakes were like diamonds
Moisture for the earth was shed.

Especially farmers, gardeners
April comes soon, time to till the soil
Plant seed, vegetables, flowers
They don't mind the labor, toil
A successful harvest produces the best
Time to ready for winter's snow next.

JOY

One may feel young at heart
Matters not what people say
Or show an envious feeling
Asking how do you spend your day.

So now at ninety years of age
My idle time is free
Praying, writing sewing baking
All a joy to me.

My fingers are not laced with diamonds
No tiaras in my hair
Clubs to keep me busy
Love surrounds me everywhere.

I would rather share a greeting
Or wave of the hand
Do something to keep busy
In this great God given land.

OLD

I could write a million words
About people I have known
From many states and countries
Kindness they have shown.

Helping celebrate my 90th
July 20, 2004
Like a glowing ember
A day to remember.

Receiving many gifts, cards, letters
Phone calls and flowers
Sending all acknowledgements
In pleasure took many hours.

May they all have memories
Keep in touch with families far away
Years pass rapidly I know
Like the sun when night ends another day.

QUESTIONS

Why, is the question,
If you have an answer give it.
When, it's time to love
This the hour live it.

Where, are you going
Who, will you see,
Questions asked each day.
What, no time to explain
Worldliness caused delay.

MISS STACEY

Good morning Miss Stacey
A greeting I'm sending today
Because you are a lovely young lady
May you always stay that way.

You enjoyed your cat that crept around
With his soft fluffy hair
He was no friend to our Schnauzer
They were not a happy pair.

Growing up a charming young lady
Helping me with garage sales
We used to laugh when over
At some of the people's wild tales.

You grew up in Chatham Illinois
Then school and work in St. Louis, Mo.
Meeting a wonderful guy named Ike
Married and off to Europe you go.

Now you're blessed with two precious boys
You brought them to visit me
Happiness has enriched your souls
Great as anyone can see.

Enjoy each day that passes
You deserve the very best
Remembering all the good times
Every time I pause to rest.

IN MEMORIAM

Another family member taken
From this earth on which we have trod.
Not our wish they leave us
Yet we know the will of God.

He sees us when we begin our life
And stands by us each day
Mary was a gracious lady
One of the best I have ever seen
Her three children are the greatest
Tom, Terry and Maureen.

We must not forget Alexa and Missy
Kevin, Andy, Morgan, Andrea and Amy too
A great granddaughter MacKenzie
Memories of life will have to do.

It was such a short time ago
Norval was called, I still wonder why
But I know he is in heaven
In God's kingdom in the sky.

So I'm sending you each an angel
Maureen, Terry, Alexa, Missy and Tom
They will offer you a prayer each day
A continuing marathon
Your mother Mary went to heaven
Close to your dad Norval's side
Led by angels watching over us
Through the grace of almighty God.

THE YATESVILLE SCHOOL

The old school house stands alone
Vacant and forlorn
Andy over we used to play
But you needed a strong arm.

There were Donovans, Bukers, Robinson
Lambkulers, Bloomfield, the Edwards clan
Henderson, Frietag, Wood and Harris
Reading, writing, arithmetic a big demand.

Hayes, Collins, Bumgardner and Summers
Attending in a one room school
Excellent teachers, I remember
Agnes Lonergan and Margaret Puhl.

We cleaned blackboards, carried in wood
For the stove to keep us warm
Drink from a tin cup that hung on the pump
Priming took a good arm.

About those by gone days
Stories each one could tell
Would bring back memories happy and sad
On which no one wants to dwell.

TERRY EDWARDS

Promising to write
About Terry, quite a lad
Alone he's an angel
With Tom around, it's bad!

Thinking you were left out of things
This really is not true
Live these young years enjoying
Because they are very few.

A masterpiece I might compose
Have it printed in the papers
About the little jokes you tell
All your other capers.

Now that summer has arrived
Play golf, swim, go fishing
Tis soon you get old me lad
It's then you'll be wishing.

You never griped about Maureen and Tom
Or the things they seem to do
Make each day a better one for yourself
Don't go around feeling blue.

Well Terry, this is your poem
May it bring a smile
Someday you will be married
Have to face those complications
That makes one's life worthwhile.

With love, Aunt Frances
Written on your 8th birthday

IN MEMORY
03-10-03

Your days were filled with happiness
And life was filled with love
When today becomes tomorrow
Someone is watching from above.

See the pleasure, hear the laughter
Many things we can enjoy
Keep your dreams, a treasure
Like a child with a new toy.

Like the quiet that surrounds you
We reached for stars on high
Hoping you would come and visit
Where the ocean meets the sky.

May you rest in peace dear Norval
Life's work on earth is done
You were such a happy person
From break of morn to set of sun.

You helped me build a garden
Of phone calls filled with mirth
With all of this accomplished
We sat down to know its worth.

So I now keep my memories
Enjoying places, meeting people
Making friends along the way
Would reach high as any steeple.

LISTEN

Hearing the sound of thundering hooves
Wind blowing in the trees
Bright sun shining on mountains and streams
Laughter to waft in the breeze.

You gave me courage, showed me the way
To listen, learn understand
I'm hoping the future will bring
Love in this wondrous land.

LIFE

We Need Faith
And must have hope
Not sit idly
To moan and grope

What happened yesterday
Is gone, refresh your mind
Greet the sunrise tomorrow
Realize life is not unkind.

LITTLE MO

Writing a relaxing pleasure
To someone we love and know
Neglect wishing you Happy Birthday
No poor excuse, I'm just slow.

Maureen you are a treasure to me
As you were to a wonderful dad
A loving brother like the others
The best friend I ever had.

Memories still come and go
Deep feelings long remain
You have many issues
And I know they cause pain

You gave concern for each parent
Doing your very best
We must go on and realize
They answered God's request.

Your dad loved you dearly
When we talked you were "Little Mo"
Show no fret, have no regret
Just let happiness overflow.

FOR MY PRIEST AND FRIEND

Congratulations Father Richard E. Grasso
Did you think all those many years ago
A vocation would call you to enter the seminary
Become a priest and reach the big four-0.

While attending St. Paul's School
Receiving the foundation for what you know
Now having touched uncountable lives
The good and dedicated sisters made it so.

You deserve the ring and plaudits
Because you give thought and inspiration
Offering praise and thanksgiving
For the people in the congregation.

So many the celebrations
At Lourdes, St. Mary's and Flagler's Maria del Mar
Were all in grateful appreciation
Like a bright and shining star.

The priests who assisted,
Fathers John O'Flaherty and John Tetlow
Years you have all served add up to many
And help make memories overflow.

So now we pray for guidance
For everyone whom you touch and know
Hoping many will be present
When you reach number five-0.

ASHLAND'S CHARLES EDWARDS FAMILY

The Charles Edwards family with dad and mom
Counted up to number ten
Frieda, Louise, Frances, also known as Ann
Charles, Tom, Norval, Russell, Robert
Were scattered all around this land.

All but Frances now passed and rest in peace
Many times tears shed over flow
Feeling each are in heaven's better place
My payers have told me so.

Memories will last and linger
As on this earth we trod
Created by the master of us all
Our Lord and Savior, almighty God.

We said goodbye to Robert
On January twenty three, 0-four
May he be received with open arms
By our great family gone before.

SMILE

Thinking I was lonesome
'Til I met a friend one day
The way she was acting
Her mind gave her away.

We chatted for a moment
Asking may we rest awhile
Answering what is important
You're not wearing any smile.

The response cam quickly
I am not feeling my best
You always have such energy
Maybe I just need some rest.

She had answered her problem
My suggestion, life is in style
Sing a song, hum a tune
Face tomorrow with a smile.

Say a little prayer today
Ease someone's pain and sorrow
The sun will shine in glory
To welcome a bright tomorrow.

IF

If you talk about your neighbor
Say a pleasant word
There is pain in each one's heart
Waiting to be heard.

Did you offer willingly
To lend a helping hand
Did you really mean it
Or maybe have a plan.

Gaining some recognition
Or want a little praise
Benefiting just yourself
Then show some mild amaze.

Well that is not called friendship
Because the path you trod
Was selfish satisfaction
And not approved by God.

CRY

Remember to be gracious
Give no reason to offend
A bouquet to shout what life is about
Faith to the last amen.

A mile the distance you travel
Smiling goes a long, long way
With zest for every season
A prayer for each day.

Memories of love, life will not fade
Store them on the shelf
Time passes quickly for everyone
Never for each one's self.

Do not be lonely, you are not
The only one left alone
Many tears shed with prayers said
Seemed days sun never shown.

Think of years we enjoyed
With family, friends by the score
The years we had were wonderful
I must not cry anymore.

HEAVEN'S GROCERY STORE

Walking down the road of life
Many years ago
Seeing one day, this sign I read
Heaven's grocery store

When I got a little closer
The door opened wide
As I approached I found myself
Walking right inside.

I saw a host of angels
Standing everywhere
One handed me a basket
Saying sweetly, shop with care.

Everything a human needed
Was in that grocery store
And if you could not carry all
They said, come back for more.

First thing I found was <u>patience</u>
With <u>love</u> in the next aisle
Next came <u>understanding</u>
An angel gave me a <u>smile</u>.

I found a box of <u>wisdom</u>
Also a bag of <u>faith</u>
I must not miss the <u>Holy Ghost</u>
Remembering I also needed <u>grace</u>.

[HEAVEN'S GROCERY STORE—continued]

One must not forget salvation
Really it's not free
Doing unto others
Will save both you and me.

I started to the counter
To pay my grocery bill
With a feeling I had everything
To do my Master's will.

As I was walking up the aisle
I saw prayer and had to add that in
Knowing when I stepped outside
I might run into sin.

Peace and joy were everywhere
Hanging from a shelf
Song and praise were also near
So I just helped myself.

Then I said to the angels
Add up how much I owe
Smiling at me they softly said
My child, God paid your bill in full
A long, long time ago.

MIRACLE

I searched for you in my dreams
Not finding you I cried
Is there no way to let you know
My love I cannot hide.

At times you seem so very near
My hopes go sailing high
I need to have you close to me
Why must you say goodbye.

Now the snow is softly falling
In flakes of billowing white
Covering each branch with beauty
What a glorious sight.

Its one of God's great miracles
A blessing that he sends
Feeding the earth with moisture
So we say amen.

ALOHA

Flowers of the islands
Greet you aloha-oi
Then those beautiful blossoms
Fade when you say goodbye.

They ask you to return to Hawaii
Knowing you will agree
When visiting such a paradise
Find friendship, love, a blue-blue sea.

They have Jasmine and Oleander
White ginger and orchids rare
The fragrance of the Plumeria
Fills the Hawaiian air.

Someday I'll return to the islands
Pick some flower with care
Give them to my sweetheart
Who is waiting for me there.

TO RUTHIE

May your days be filled with happiness
Your life full of love
So when today becomes tomorrow
Someone is watching from above.

See the pleasure, hear the laughter
There was much we did enjoy
We had dreams and we shared treasures
Like children with a new toy.

Now as quiet time surrounds you
Reach for stars that shine on high
Never fret for God is with you
And he hears your every sigh.

LONELY

Walk along a lonely road
Find peace in every step
Pause and think how lonely
Our Lord was when he wept.

TO TERRY & MISSY

Frown not about the things you hear
Smile as you go along
Let the beauty that surrounds you
Leave a feeling that you belong.

Seek not the path of failure
Look around with wonder
Why following each lightning strike
Comes the roar of thunder.

You live in California
We're in Florida close to the sea
You have earthquakes; we have hurricanes
Part of God's great mystery.

You have mountains, ocean and deserts
We have forests, cities and sand
What a grand and glorious mixture
We find in this wonderful land.

Let us each be willing
Give a moment or two each day
Trying to help the unfortunate
Traveling along life's way.

OF CARL

I do not think it strange at all
They found Carl on the floor
He heard someone call to him
Appearing at his hospital room door.

His angel touched him gently
He arose with style and grace
A miracle he saw Frieda and his angel
Standing there smiles on their face.

The moment that he saw her
His angel smiled with love
They had come to take him with them
To live in heaven above.

Yes I believe in angels
They are around us everywhere
When we reach out our hand
Our families angels will be there.

So please do not fret, have no regret
When tears come let them flow
Each one shed an angel said
A prayer to make our memories grow.

HOBBY

Ask forgiveness if you hurt
A small thing to do
Saying you are sorry
Creates a friendship tried and true.

Many times in life you're thinking
Things have passed you by
Share some greetings, be happy
Good thoughts lift you to the sky.

Poetry is a hobby
I enjoy to fullest measure
Putting words on paper
Hoping someone will treasure

Expressing thoughts loving living
Being thankful this I pray
Caring for the need of others
Might brighten a cloudy day

Be a friend each day that passes
Reach out be not afraid
Stand out one of the masses
Life is worth the price you paid.

MY AGE

Being all alone can get lonely
Just wait a few more years
Think you are the one and only
Be happy, erase any sign of tears.

As older we get, less we do and see
Tempers grow short I must agree
Showing anger or frustration
Little things said cause accusation.

When your ideas mean nothing
Growing old not a thrill
Have a good time, why worry or fret
They too will age, this you can bet.

Just say a prayer for someone
Be brave, let happiness flow
Laughter helps lighten the load
Years cause footsteps to slow.

TO MARVIN FROM ANITA

I love you Marvin Allessee
And the years we have together
You're my knight in shining armor
In any kind of weather.

From the day I first met you
Dressed in style a smiling face
You called me "Dear Anita:
My heart began to race.

Oh these happy days together
They will never leave my mind
Our love molded us together
As a leaf clings to a vine.

Traveling miles to foreign places
Seeing sights in this great land
Enjoying people, conversations
Reaching out a gracious hand.

Now we've traveled life's great highways
Reaching out from shore to shore
You protected me from all danger
My love is yours forevermore.

Frances made a promise
To write for me some work
I know her promise will be kept
A duty she would not shirk.

I will thank her when I'm better
And present this poem to you

Filled with all my love and feelings
For a man so tried and true.

Please take care my "Darling Marvin"
Enjoy life at its best
I will always be your sweetheart
Greeting family, friend or guest.

Written 1995

MCKENZIE

There is a little girl named McKenzie
Whom I have not met and do not know
I know her mom and grandparents
And where they live
In a suburb of San Diego.

Her mother's name is Andrea,
Grandma Missy (Nanna) Grandpa Terry (Grampy)
I've known him from a baby
When at times he could be cranky.

Recently Terry and Missy came to visit
Where ocean meets the sky for miles
In the great state of Florida
Visitors leave with many smiles.

Some day McKenzie you might come to visit
Swim in our backyard pool
Visit the beach and pick up shells
For show and tell when going to school.

Have a happy time each day you live
Playing and doing fun things
Aunt Maureen can play the Guitar
Michael row the boat ashore
And all the others sing.

Aunt Frances, May 2004

A NEW DAY

Start each day with a smile
Even though you might feel sad
The sun shines dispels the gray
Then you won't feel bad.

Have yourself a cup of coffee
Or whatever drink you choose
Putter around with little duties
What have you got to lose.

Get in the car, go shopping
To the dollar store
Say hello to someone you meet
Feel better, why ask for more

When the sun is setting
As daylight starts to fade
Feel secure never doubt
The progress you have made.

PAUSE

Driving down a highway, slow or fast
Someone behind you gives his horn a blast
Slow down, never look aghast
Just let the idiot pass.

COME BACK TOMORROW

You have gone and left me
I get lonely every day
Darling I keep hoping
You'll come back to me someday.

We wanted home and family
When you sent away to serve
For our grand old country
And you never lost your nerve.

Come back tomorrow my darling
Always my wish will be
You will get tired of wandering and
Come back tomorrow to me.

SEARCH

We owe our very life to Him
From which we must not turn
Sharing, loving, caring
Never fail to show concern.

Hoping to be remembered
Doing a good deed
Keep on trying, do not give up
Find someone in need.

Reach out each and everyday
Say a little prayer
When the search is over
Find one who will care.

PRAY

Holy Mary mother mine
Hurt I caused many a time
You told me kneel, pray
The master forgives in everyway.

FREE

Blessed mother you gave me
Ideas for feeling free.

BROTHER NORVAL

I know the pain you suffered
And the tears each day you shed
Hoping God was ever with you
Each day my prayers were said.

Even all the friends around you
Showed their willingness to share
You smiled through your sadness
With pain impossible to bear.

We know God was listening
Gave you a chance to smile again
Be happy, share your heaven
Your agony was not in vain.

MY DOOR

Reaching out
I held your hand
When knocking
On my door
You whispered
Please be my friend
I will be grateful
Evermore.

FRIEND

Many times I sit and ponder
About things I might have done
Spent more them helping others
Shared some laughter, had more fun.

When at times you feel like crying
Knowing not what lies in store
Look around if there is sadness
Give a smile, don't close the door.

Make a day for someone brighter
Each of us has felt some pain
If a friend has misfortune
Show cause to smile again.

Would you walk a mile
In their footsteps
As they struggled on the way
Or would you really help them
Saying rest awhile and pray.

Then we will travel together
Reaching out to hold their hand
You may find your burden lighter
Then each will understand.

BROTHER TOM

Years have passed, memories linger
Like a burning flame.
In silent meditation a prayer is said
For one who sought no fame.

Giving strength, help to everyone
This kind and gentle man
Good he did will surely live
With people across this land.

Happy memories remain
Life goes on you see
Grief must not linger, this he said
Live the future beautifully.

JOY

If tomorrow brings joy
Like yesterday gave
Share good things of life
Open your arms to love
Offer a future without strife
My wish for everyone
Enjoying each beautiful dawn.

GOOD THINGS

If tomorrow brings happiness
Like yesterday gave
May I share good things of life
Open my arms to a loved one
Live a future without strife.
My wish for everyone
Enjoy each beautiful dawn
See a child held in his mother's arms
Tell us, life must go on

KNOWING

I know strength, wisdom and love
Will make the stairway to heaven
Easier to climb.

TRY

I watched the night
Turn into day
Saw stars and moon
Give way to sun
Brighten up our day.

The earth alive
With living things
Birds that sing
A cloudless sky
Each may well give pleasure
If only we will try;

Do a good deed for someone
Give them a reason to smile
Sharing, caring, loving
You will be in style.

Never feel the day
Is not worthwhile
Share sadness, you may see
Being kind is magic
The angels all agree.

WISHING

Give us faith to live and learn
As through each day we trod
Remembering always in all ways
It's with the help of God.

Wander down a lonely path
Find joy and happiness
Look up at the blue of sky
We have so much to bless.

Turn around and wander back
The path we left behind
Realizing there is someone
To whom we must be kind.

Lend a hand, say a prayer
Hoping they will hear
Voices of angels floating by
Because they are always near.

RECIPE

A pound of energy
Pinch of imagination
Knack for understanding
A kettle of information.

WILLINGLY

Thinking if I tried willingly
To lend a helping hand
You might feel some pleasure
Perhaps then understand

Living can be beautiful
And the pathway easy we trod
By caring, loving, sharing
All with the help of God.

If you let despair and loneliness
Follow wherever you go
The road to peaceful living
Will never be easy I know.

Remember others have known heartache
This road you don't travel alone
They found the way to happiness
By the good seed they have sown.

TRY

Try to gain—never waste
A moment of the day
There is someone watching
Hasten, do not delay
Each step you take
Share a smile
For a heart
About to break

THINK ABOUT IT

One has to work at friendships
As in a garden filled with flowers
Unless you want the weeds to grow
And spoil the many hours
You spent in weeding, feeding
Those tender little seeds
Like a moment taken
Doing countless friendly deeds.

We cannot live on make believe
Even though our dreams add beauty
Sharing precious memories
Brings happiness not duty
May we each let friendship grow
By reaching out a hand
Extend it to a neighbor
Across this wondrous land.

Plant some flowers, sow those seeds
Learn to be forgiving
Even though times we hurt
Its great to be living
Need some help, ask for it
God will hear your plea
Smile to show how gracious
He forgives with T.L.C.

WITH LOVE TO TOM

His name not known for wealth or fame
Around this great big earth
Yet we loved him very much
Since the first day of his birth.

You called him, Master of us all
To your kingdom for his rest
He will pray for us poor sinners
Because in heaven he is blessed.

Loving his family, sisters, brothers
Brought joy to all he knew
Memories of his loving ways
His years were all too few.

His life was lived in doing
From dawn to set of sun
For God and all acquaintances
Still found some time for fun.

May he be given a golden crown
Many things he did without credit
Brothers like Tom we miss so much
Always we'll be indebted.

SMILE

Something to cherish
Almost everyday you live
There are good and not so good days
We must take as well as give

Everyone has problems sometimes
Let not your anger show
Live and laugh at little nothings
Every time you are tempted
Never let anguish show.

There will be things in life
Everyone has tasks to face
Talk over the various chores
Each can help these jobs erase.

Find what gives you pleasure
Everyday that passes by
Smile, fill your life with treasure
Hold your head up to the sky.

GOD'S GIFTS 1969

Happiness is maple leaves
Falling in the gentle breeze
Sparkling in the misty dawn
Lying silent on the lawn.

See the stream so glistening
Hear the crickets listening
Tiny new born rabbits scurry
Always in a hurry.

Bright eyed woodchucks hear their whistle
Catch the purple of a thistle
The red cardinal still hangs around
Eating morsels from the ground.

Summer in its brilliance glows
All to soon the winter snows
Shrouds us in winter white
Sparkling in the moon filled night.

Thanksgiving time soon comes 'round
Fruits, acorns and chrysanthemums abound
Burning leaves, smoke fills the air
There is beauty everywhere.

DAWN 1997

Let us celebrate
Adventure enjoyed today
Dawn comes each tomorrow
Summer isn't far away
Leaving no time for sorrow.

Mother's day arrives in may
Father's day in June
The July 4 celebrations
Appear very soon
Fly the flag, show your pride
T'is not a day for gloom
Make each dawn worthwhile
Traveling that extra mile.

BE KIND

Searching years you may never find
Luck, some have all the time
You know moments of pleasure
Teaching others to be kind.

LIFE

Life is not a game of chance
You bet on and hope to win
So when there is a problem
Just take it on the chin.

We have things that irritate
Through each day we go
Be yourself, don't overact
By putting on a show.

When it comes to learning
Do your very best
The important thing is knowledge
For you to pass the test.

Life is given to we humans
Let's show the world we're proud
If only a little something
With gusto shout aloud.

Help someone less fortunate
Lend a hand when they are down
Share a smile, walk that mile
You will erase a frown.

FRIENDS

There is no doubt
I'd like to shout
About some friends I know
Who do for others constantly
But never putting on a show.

Their outstretched hands
Are reaching out
For anyone in need
And it does not matter
Color, race or creed.

These are people
We call friends
Who said they are few
They share our fame
Our joy and pain
Are dear and forever true.

DREAMS

May days be filled with happiness
Your life full of love
When today becomes tomorrow
Someone's watching from above.

See the pleasure, hear the laughter
There was much we did enjoy
Dreams we shared were treasured
Like a child with a new toy.

Now quiet time surrounds me
Like the stars that shine on high
I will not fret or show regret
The master hears my every sigh.

OUR TROOPS

You live to love not deceive
Never be jealous or show any greed
So take time, relax then pause
Not anger without cause.

Our land is freedom country
Red, white and blue we proudly wave
We unite with all our might
To remain strong and brave.

It seems not right to see the troops
Traveling to distant shores
Yet to protect the USA
They were gathered by the scores.

Some places have wars for ages
We should let them fight their way
Because many of the USA courageous
May not live another day.

AUTUMN

Autumn is upon us
School soon begun
My wish for all
Try to learn
Get along with everyone
Enjoy the sports
Have lots of fun.

INVITE

Stephanie, Chelsea, Callahan and Joe
Great grandchildren I love to know
Do your best, pass each test
When time comes, let there be no hesitation
Send me a graduation invitation.

REACH

Longing Lord to hear your prayers
Teach me no more to sin
Reach out, grasp my weary heart
Fold me close within.

Reach in faith, reach in love
Reach, reach out your arm
Accept me kind and gracious God
Who keeps all from harm.

Reach out and see the hand of one
Standing beside you now
I reached out you helped me
So I make a vow
To serve, share, understand
Each day that I shall live
When a sinner asks
A willing God forgives.

We each need strength
All must love
Have patience as we trod
Truth and knowledge we receive
From a kind and gracious God.

CRY NO MORE

My childhood was filled with pleasures
I wondered what the future held in store
Seems my days are filled with dreams
I need not cry anymore.

Now a future we plan together
Things passed out of our life.
Being together in all weather
Bring freedom from all trouble and strife.

Church bells resound with a message
Lifting my eyes to implore
Rest of years, you share fears
I need not cry anymore.

May faith never leave
God has opened the door
He stays by our side to comfort and guide
We need never cry anymore.

Never close your eyes to sadness
Reach a loving hand
Friendship the answer
Gentle like a grain of sand.
When you reach there's magic
Some pleasure you might bring
A smile someone might treasure
Like a sunny day in spring.

HOLD ME JOE

Hold me in your arms I may share
Part of a wonderful life
Love has been so beautiful
Since we became husband and wife.

Of course we're not growing younger
Let not it be said we are old
There's much to be enjoyed
When loving a hundred fold.

Please open your arms, give hope
Be friend to someone lonely
Seeing them smile is worthwhile
Joe you're the one and only.

LET US GROW

Knowledge lets us grow
Gaining wisdom has no rules
Never try fighting it
Ignorance was made for fools.

Each of has have known sadness
May we never forget to pray
The burden will seem lighter
The end of a trying day.

Did you know that heartache
Causes pain deep within
When turning your back on anyone
You never expect to win.

Fame nor fortune not my aim
But friends more than coins of gold
Why is it one often hears
Excuse them, they're getting old.

May I never turn away
From anyone in need
Sometime I might ask for help
Praying someone will intercede.

CRESTVIEW DRIVE

When arising in the morning
A vision from your dreams
Amid quiet and peaceful surroundings
Day dawns on hillside and streams.

Just see the sunrise o'er Crestview Drive
As dew from the lawn disappears
A heart filled with love for everyone
Finds no place for sadness or fears.

I loved our home on Crestview Drive
All the family and friends with whom we shared
Though nothing lasts forever
Everyone touched knows how much we cared.

RICK

A lad with such a zest for life
Keeps me on the run
Not quiet for a minute
From dawn to set of sun.

Over night he wants to stay
'cause home is not too far away
Then comes next morn clear and bright
Hey, can I stay again tonight.

First outside, then comes in
Grandma, is it time to eat again
Me get lonesome, how could this be
When grandson Rick comes to stay with me.

THE SUN

The sun may cast a shadow
Of a human such as me
A kind word softly spoken
Reaps a harvest
And it's free.

UNLESS

Words on paper
Meaningless things
Unless they're full of love
And play on heartstrings.

LOOK UP

When you see
A smiling face
Show happiness
Open your arms
Give a fond embrace.

WITH PRIDE

Offering my love will you accept
I'm giving it with pride
Promise you won't turn away
You're needed at my side.

Things in past forgotten
We must live today
If there is gossip, who cares
Some folks have little to say.

Hold out your hand, come into my arms
Kiss me darling again
Thinking about you fills each day
Forget heartache and pain.

A song of gladness brings rich memories
That I never shall forget
Tunes you hummed soft and tender
Not a day I regret.

If by chance I prosper
Always caring a must
Never forgetting
God has given faith and trust.

Rich in health and understanding
Right to worship as I may
He has never been demanding
A promise he keeps everyday.

CHIMES

Chimes from the Cathedral
Remind me of Rome
Things, places and people
We meet away from home.

Memories keep returning
Of a promise and a vow
No matter what the reason
We forgave you anyhow.

A month, a day, you stayed away
Loving you, we missed your smile
The long awaited letter came
I'll be home after while.

Cathedral chimes ring out anew
I'm praying they will bring
You safely back to loving arms
Now that it is spring.

RAINBOW

Clear like a pool of water
Aglow after a summer rain
Rainbow on high spanning the sky
A lingering refrain.

The rainbow is God's creation
In fairy tales told
By searching at the end of it
We'll find a pot of gold.

Colors of orange, pink and violet
A marvel to view after rain
Like a loved ones returning
To a heart that's yearning
May the rainbow of love remain.

MEASURE

A single pound of energy
Added to a mile of smiles
Mixed with a cup of determination
Will make a day worthwhile.

My back aches, my head hurts
There is a pain in my toe
But a third cup of laughter
Is better than complaining, you know.

With a half cup of pep
Good thoughts by the dozen
Not for sale the wave of hand
A telephone call, a spoonful of pleasure
Worth a hundred pounds of sand.

So let the good sense God gave you
Give you that ounce of inspiration
With a pinch of salt remember
A barrel of hope the best foundation.

RAIN

Gentle rain began to fall
On earth so dry
Very soon the say seemed brighter
Need you ask why
New life was given to living things
Trees awoke started listening
Their branches shook with pride
Because we know without the gift
Of showers from above
All life will fade to nothingness
Along with love.

I HEARD

I heard you asking me to come home
Being away from faith, I seemed to roam
Seeing no future I needed a guide
Suddenly you were there at my side

REJOICE

Seeing your smile, hearing your voice
Gave me reason to rejoice
Doing as you promised
Stopping to take my hand
On that sunny day long ago
You made life just grand.

FOR US

You shared your life, shared your love
Died so many might know
A sinner will not be abandoned
Our faith has taught us so.

GLOW

Light a candle as it burns
The tiny flame will glow
To brighten up the pathway
Of someone feeling low.

YOU

Happiness could be remembering today
You helped someone along the way
If only time to share a smile
Their day perhaps was more worthwhile

Never let them see you frown
It might turn their day upside down
A promise kept is worthwhile
Helps them walk that extra mile.

HOPE

Being thankful every morning
When the sun comes out to shine
Today I must think of others
With problems on their mind.

Call them on the telephone
Someone lonely or sad
My daily work not important
Better that some ever had.

Brighten their day give a friendly hello
Or smile if they pass you by
The burden will be less heavy
Shall we give hope a try.

THE ROAD

We each travel the road to happiness
Ambition a principal thing
The beauty of living surrounds us
Especially in the spring.

ONCE IN A WHILE

To keep a friend
Kindness is needed
Thoughtfulness heeded
Honor them with a smile
Walk life together
Once in awhile
In all you do, be honest and true
Happiness will last
As you travel each mile.

WISE

Be it Easter, Christmas or New Years Day
Will you try to make friends
Easing the pain of a loved one
Make them feel like living again.

Being gracious wherever going
Kind in thought and deed
Stay with someone in trouble
Plant a prayerful seed.

Small enough to take their place
Wise enough to show
Believe in what they are doing
And want the world to know.

A better person you might be
When showing that you care
Give of yourself helping others
God is always there.

HAIL MARY

Hail Mary in heaven
Pray to Jesus for me.
If worthy, I'm asking please
Pray for sinners
Bring back those who stray.
May I be forgiven
When failing to say, thank you sweet Jesus
For a wonderful day.

JOY

Joy is found in doing
Over and over again
Happiness is worth pursuing
When easing someone's pain.

MY DAY

I saw you this morning
You made me smile
Then the rest of my day
Was really worthwhile.

VISIT ME

Come visit on a cloudy day
Or when the sun in bright
Sharing some happy times
Will be sheer delight

If the clouds play peek-a-boo
When the moon is in the sky
I welcome you with open arms
At least its worth a try.

APPLAUSE

I offer you good things in life
And if you have a whim
Be it filled with sharing
Then the darkness will dim.

No one could be more worthy
Constantly you volunteer
This toast we drink to you my friend
Heartfelt and most sincere.

Getting along with fellowmen
For each and every cause
Here's wishing you the very best
Stand, receive applause.

CARES

Sitting alone one evening
Cares of the day are past
Wishing joy and peace for everyone
May their happiness always last.

STREAMS

The small stream flows gently
Across green pastures where cattle graze
Slowly quietly winding its way
Into a massive lake where people gaze.

In sail or speedboats folks are having fun
Shedding cares in the summer sun
After rains the stream runs full
If thinking we might agree
Almost like magic understanding
A world full of joy and free.

IMAGINATION

Sitting by the window looking out
Seeing nothing, but in my imagination
I heard someone at the door.
My thoughts go wandering
Dreams are not expensive things
Perhaps I should get busy, sweep the floor.

Then came a call by telephone
Asking if I were alone
Could someone stop to see me
As they were passing my home
Quickly did I realize
It was a pleasant surprise
You can always share some happiness
Imagination is inspiring
Once you've given it a try.

I NEED YOU LORD

I need your love
To keep me strong
Need you beside me
When doing wrong.

Think everyday
You're near in everyway
With your help
I will not stray.

ALL THINGS

Beautiful as the silence
Swift like the flowing streams
Bright when the sun in shining
Touched by angel's wings.

Clear green eyes that sparkle
As they look at a sleeping babe
Dainty as rain splashed puddles
Just as a blossom they fade.

Cool like a day in springtime
Sharp as the morning breeze
Pale as an echo repeating
Whispering through the trees.

Like gossamer wings all these things
With prayer, make a beautiful life
Dreams are free so we agree
Not feel anger or strife.

MEMORY BOOK

There are friendships we cherish
As we travel on life's way
Often shall we recollect
Good times we've filed away.

Gather sunshine like the roses
Moist with dew each blade of grass
Let the golden rule surround you
Not an idle hour pass.

Don't throw away that memory book
Think back on happy years
You'll find life has been beautiful
Then smile away your tears.

NO WAY

Without the mighty
Hand of God
Watching over me
It would be impossible
To enjoy eternity.

SOPHIA

A friend to be remembered
Through life she learned to give
Shared her intelligence with many
What better way to live.

Leaving memories and a legend
For each to appreciate
Saying never show your ignorance
A good listener proves you are great.

Never complained of being burdened
Had her problems like the rest
When you saw Sophia smiling
Knew you had passed the best.

REASONING

Loving brings a glow to each one's life
Caring helps end problems and strife
Giving adds hours of pleasure
Contains something to measure.

Just show someone how much you care
Willing always, do your share
Hoping that each tomorrow might bring
Reasoning and understanding for each small thing.

LITTLE ONE

Little candle, little light
Lots of hope in waiting
Shine a light of happiness
On those anticipating.

LISTEN

Listen to what I tell you
The world is a wonderful place
When kindness is shown to others
A harvest of love you embrace.

If sometime you are weary
Feel life has let you down
Listen, someone is saying
Please don't wear a frown.

Hark, someone is whispering
We all have cares, come what may
By listening to a friend's problem
You have brightened their day.

RAPTURE

I shall whisper a sweet nothing
Each time you hold me close
If there is little meaning
Being near you counts the most.

Seeing you each day a pleasure
The way you shown concern
Wishing to make you happy
There is much we learn.

With each hour and day that passes
I enjoy with sheer delight
Hoping when tomorrow dawns
Things planned come out right.

THINKING

Sitting alone in the evening
Cares of the day are past
Wishing joy for everyone
Wanting happiness to last.

Like romantic lovers holding hands
Watching children at play
All these things contentment brings
Now I put problems away.

RISEN

At the stroke of midnight
We know He is risen
Such agony he suffered
In the darkened prison.

If faith we have
His love will win
Knowing that each believe
The divine master of us all
Gave blessings to receive.

Thankful for this we
Show appreciation
May we never fail to kneel
In wondrous adoration.

Someone mighty made this world
To serve the human race
Giving strength and courage
When problems we might face.

Search no longer friend
Have faith, do your best
The heavy cross He carried
Put Him to the test.

Now when the bells ring out
We know that He is risen
His sufferings were for everyone
Through this we be forgiven.

A LETTER

Sitting in church listening
To a letter from Bishop Joe
Telling of Lenten regulations
Something Catholics should know.

Sacrifice something we enjoy
Giving up a pleasure
Fill the rice bowl to the top
For less fortunate to treasure.

Living in the land of plenty
Believing in the golden rule
When not doing for others
We just play the fool.

They say prayers can move mountains
A dam can stop a river's flow
Enchantment of life is beautiful
Because God told us so.

Help the weary along the road
When the day was long
When we rested He was there
Giving strength to make us strong.

We bow our heads asking forgiveness
He will not turn away
Just keeps reaching out, lost souls to gain
Hoping no more will stray.

Whisper amen at the end of prayer
Even though hastily said
He listens, hears each faint request
Worthy each day ahead.

NEVER DESPAIR

If we ask will there by answers
To questions that fill our minds
Everyone has a scheme, often dream
Of a fortune they might find

Reach out, grasp love, hold it close
From days beginning to end
Never despair, God is there
And will always be your friend.

LITTLE PRAYER

Idle words are not for me
When whispering a prayer
Even when foolishness creeps in between
I know that you are there.

DOCTOR QUOTE

'tis not a joke
You shorten your life
the longer you smoke.

LE CAT

Le Cat is a crazy thing
Black as charcoal ink
Jumps from chair to windowsill
Quicker than a wink.

Just a scrawny little thing
When Timmy brought her home
Getting her for his birthday
When someone let her roam.

Now she's grown into a beauty
Knowing right from wrong
Drives the dogs most crazy
Chases lizards all day long.

I guess that we will keep Le Cat
Though sometimes its not funny
Especially when she decided to eat
The chocolate Easter bunny.

ALOUD

Be funny
Make someone smile
Then laugh aloud
Very worthwhile.

AWAKE

Awake to the beauty of morning
Previous days troubles behind
Say hello to neighbor and friend
Never show you're unkind,

Put on a smile get outside
Look around at growing things
The earth abounds in loveliness
In wonderful glorious spring.

Enjoyment brings hours of pleasure
Busy hands make time fly
A little prayer is a treasure
Rewarding each, if we try,

Awake to the beauty of loving
Holding a life in your hand
Have regard for everyone
You meet in this wondrous land.

To me 'tis like a flower
Opened to suns rays
Especially when time passes
I've lived many days.
Then you called me on the phone
One day to say hello
The entire day seemed brighter
For someone feeling low.

RULES

I intend not worry ever
About rules when being bent
Just keep right in there working
Hoping each hour will be spent.

In a good deed helping others
Find the sun's bright rays
Wishing that the hand of God
Made easier their ways.

Laughter could be the answer
A smile is on our face
The day could be worth living
Problems easier to erase.

THE BEST

Be happy with living, learn to laugh
Don't let anything stand in the way
Look around at all the beauty
Facing you each day.
Should there be problems, help make amends
It could be a stranger or friend
Comes the time need not be sad
Know that you've given
The best you had.

HEARTBREAK LANE

I ask once more, will you forgive _
I did not want to cause you pain
You found a love that's new
Left me sad and blue.
Now I'll walk alone down heartbreak lane.
Wishing the very best in life for you dear
Since you're leaving, I: must remain.
Remember when you go
My love was true and so
Memories overflow, in heartbreak lane
Please go, may I forget you
The storm clouds bring the rain
Reminds me of the day we met
Now I must forget
Walk alone down heartbreak lane.

CLOSE

Thinking about you during the day
And oft times at night
Not really sure I must confess
It almost gives me fright
Never thinking the time would come
When I wanted someone to be
Beside me the rest of my life
So all the world could see.

TRY

Prayer answered each who try
Giving help along the way
Kindest words cost nothing
They're ours to use each day.

Just making someone happy
Takes a few short minutes
Loving praying, doing
Put some effort in it.

Lets try our best, pass the test
Really care, show some pride
There is more to life than take, my friend
Let conscience be your guide.

PEACE AND LOVE

Peace and love be to those
When suffering any loss
Excuse the overbearing
The angry, mean and cross.

BROTHER CHARLES 1987

You know I really loved you
Even when you caused me pain
With all the broken promises
I did my best to remain.

A friend through those bad times
When pain dwells within
Praising not the answer
I did that time and time again.
Again dear Lord I'm asking
Keep his feet upon the ground
Prayer is the answer
With you it can be found.

THE SHADOW

The shadow of doubt disappeared from view
When I looked and saw your smile
Right then I knew how willing
Walking that extra mile.

LITTLE PRAYER

Idle words are not for me
When whispering a prayer
Even when foolishness creeps in between
I know that you are there.

JOE

I started you a letter
Took a minute out to pray
Tears were blotting out the words
When thinking of yesterday,

We had spoken of our love
Planned things along the way
Now alone, I think about
Promises of yesterday.

Hearing friends speak of tomorrow
They seem happy and carefree
I close my eyes and whisper
That won't be for you and me,

Must dry the tears and start again
Have courage not to cry
By keeping all the memories
Idle hours go swiftly by.

NETA

You are a beautiful person
Giving time whenever needed
Helping one less fortunate
In this you have succeeded,

Making people smile through their tears
Bringing joy to those you meet
Doing all these little things
A basket of love I place at your feet.

A TIME

If you think there is a time
When prayer does not matter
Sow some seeds of kindness
Surely they will scatter.

The wind will blow them all around
Where they should be sewn
What matters is the prayerful way
They thrive until full grown.

THE ROSE

Seeing beauty in the petals
Of the rose you gave to me
May the fragrance always linger
Especially in my memory.

FAULTS

Try sincerely some faults to erase
Sow seeds of kindness, enjoy an embrace
Consideration can be shown
As each day passes by
Sheer contentment will soothe
Just like a lullaby.

ATONEMENT

We know the agony
Our Lord suffered on the cross
We have the knowledge given a chance
Atone for His bitter loss.

Still giving blessings to evil ones
Should make us stop and pray
Wishing for each a better world
Live and love every way.

WISDOM

There is a road to happiness
Find it along the way
Traveling the path of wisdom
Don't throw a life away,

God always caring protects us
As we roam around this land
Know by asking he never neglects
Reaching out a helping hand.

HELLO GOODBYE

Hello-goodbye what's in a word
Meaning without end
A cheery card a harvest of love
Sent to a longtime friend.

Saying goodbye might give pain
Its better to express
Say hello, make someone's life glow
Add to your success.

CLOSE

You held out your arms to me
Being the man of my dreams
Now my heart is lighter
Days are brighter
Having loved you forever it seems
Are you ready for me to confess
There is no other one
Open your arms hold me close
There will always be a sun
Shining on lovers such as we
Even though in our golden years
We plan a future together
Put away all fears.

DELIGHT

One step closer to being mine
An inch nearer to love
A mile walked together
With a million stars above,
I measure a yard of happiness
A score of moon beams bright
Stretching out my arms for love
Will bring sheer delight.

LADY IN BLUE

Just a dream I hold in my heart
Your beauty a memory
Although we are miles apart
I see you lady in blue

Very soon you will learn dear
My love is everlasting
This promise was made long ago
So once again I'm asking,

Though the ocean is between us
When you say I will depart
Stay close beside you always
You have the key to my heart,

No more then to wander
Because near you I remain
Lady in blue my love is true
Praying you feel the same.

MISS YOU

Miss being with you
Holding you close
Need you here in my arms
Think about you during the day
At night dream of your charms,
When days are long I get lonesome
Must keep myself occupied
Want to be with you forever
Couldn't forget if I tried.

RETIRING

We all have dreams of retiring
To enjoy life filled with zest
Talk about places where we might go
Some choose the glorious west,

A home on the outskirts of Saint Louie
Or the seashore where sandpipers roam
Quiet of a small country village
Place I decide to call home.

View mountains, sail oceans, visit foreign lands
A place to find relaxation
The swimming pool in my back yard
A great place for conversation.

When everyone comes to visit
Friends, family, neighbors stop by
Children with all the games they play
Lift your thoughts to the sky.

Sure I've traveled and really enjoyed
Visiting the foreign nations
Still it's good to be at home
To hold a celebration.

When you retire don't rush around
As though there is no tomorrow
Share good times with those you love
Leaving no time for sorrow.

LITTLE THINGS

What are the little things in life
A smile a laugh a sigh
Not something taken for granted
Let never a day pass by,

Little things are important
Like a compliment or such
Whispering a tiny secret
To one you love so much,

Listen someone might be calling
With news you have been expecting
These are the little things.
Giving life special zing.

I BELIEVE

Being a friend, showing love
brings everlasting happiness.

COULD BE

Today is what yesterday was, only better.

HOME

A place with care and tenderness
Blessing each who dwell within
Spreading happiness sharing laughter
And a chance to win.

Kindness shown by others
In so many ways
Sometimes a laugh to cherish
Even on the darkest days,

A home is where you will find
Lots of love around
A home is where when someone strays
May they soon be homeward bound.

BEAUTY

Beauty is a thing to cherish
Knowing this we must agree
If you smile your eyes will sparkle
So remember you and me,

To enhance looks keep on buying
What comes in bottles, tubes and jars
Real beauty is deep within
Just being what we are.

True we all rely on makeup
For our cheeks our eyes and lips
Special creams to hide the wrinkles
Polish toenails and fingertips,

Some give praise to the beautician
The many hours she spent
Though not raving beauties
We must smile and be content.

NOT FORSAKEN

I will always love you darling
Even though you've ceased to care
Think of me with kindness
When a moment you might spare.

Why is it the good times
Seem to pass me by
You were acting evil
And causing me to cry.

Foolish when I shed the tears
That belong to loneliness
All I wanted was your love
Not to feel distress.

I must wake up and look around
Stupid I would be
I am not forsaken
Because god loves me for free.

I owe my very life to Him
Away, I shall not turn
Just go on loving you my sweet
Though you show no concern.

May the saints in all their wisdom
Let me never feel depressed
Keep me searching for the goodness
Which leaves no time for guess.

I shall reach out everyday
Wishing all that's good

And when my day is ended
I will be understood.

Because prayer is the answer
And faith a precious seed
Wisdom is the knowledge
Given hope we can succeed.

A LITTLE SOMETHING

Let a day not pass without doing
Good deeds along the way
Matters not if something big
Just help someone have a good day.

Each deed can be beautiful
We have a lot to learn
Whenever doing for others
The Master shows great concern.

Many people need a kind word
Show them you really care
Stop and visit a shut-in
Spread some sunshine there.

Return home tired and happy
Knowing today you have trod
The path of joy doing
A little something for God.

NIGHT

It is evening and the dark of night
Like a curtain,
Casts a shadow on my dreams.

RELAX

Peace will come to those who grasp
The first rays of the morning sun
Then relax at end of day
See their tasks well done.

THIS LAND

Wind is good for a sailboat
Warm sun brings spring flowers
Seasons, with all kinds of weather
We need in this land of ours,

A friendly hello a beautiful thing
Shared with someone sad
It will give us happiness
Making them feel glad.

This land for people may they believe
There is a better tomorrow
Filled with joy and pleasure
To chase away their sorrow.

WHY NOT

Why not reach out for happiness
What harm could there be
Making someone smile is so worthwhile
Because it happened to me.

YOU AND ME

Think life is like a fading rose
How foolish can you be
There is someone watching
Supporting you and me.
May a million prayers outnumber
The footsteps I have trod
And the sun shine even brighter
When one who strayed returns to God.

MY HAND

Please won't you share happiness
What harm could there be
When I reach out, will you take my hand
My friendship is free.

And then perhaps should you need
My help in your sorrow
I will reach out offering my hand
Tomorrow, tomorrow, tomorrow.

The past behind us the present here
Ease for their sorrow
Some people may live for today
From them I wish to borrow.

A chance to say, I knew yesterday
Yet willingly let it slip by
Not caring so much of getting in touch
With one who had reason to cry.

When it's said there's a future ahead
I have the chance again
To live this day, lovingly pray
My memories will long remain.

TOUCH OF LOVE
JOE 1931

Your touch of love has finally found
This heart of mine
I used to envy everyone
Their life and love so fine.

Then by chance the other day
You walked across the street
You were the touch of love I needed
To make my life complete.

Seems as though the guiding hand
Of a power up above
Had been forever waiting
To see our touch of love.

You're the one I have been wanting
For many lonely years
Forgive my darling while I pause
And brush away the tears.

Thinking the greatest joys of life
Had surely passed me by
Like the weary traveler
I no longer seemed to try.

Then behold the choir of angels
Was singing in heaven above
Across the street, I ran to me
My own true touch of love.

4255 MAYFAIR LANE

Harlan has a new home
In Florida's Port Orange
Moving here from Illinois
Quite a good dramatic change.

No more freezing weather
Or scooping snow and blustering wind
It took a while for him to say
I'm going to pack and move away.

No more salt for icy streets
Or heavy blankets over sheets
Put away those extra heavy clothes
And woolen socks for frozen toes.

Friend Harlan, welcome to
The Sunshine State
When you're moved in
Invite us, we'll help you celebrate.

LEARN

Please do not be heartbroken
Give a friendly smile
The road will seem less bumpy
Even though you walked a mile.

How long were you wandering
Searching new life afar
In a sea you're floundering
Wishing on a star.

Come down to earth it's beautiful
There is much to treasure
Frowning causes wrinkles
Deep enough to measure.

Never grow old without living
Everyday at its best
Learn, be forgiving
Then you will e'er be blessed.

GIFT

Listen to me
My love is free
May I give it to you
Promises my pet
Will bring regret
If not meant to be true.

NO FEAR

The future of what lies ahead
Even though in your golden years
Little prayers often said
Chase away all fears.

So I write about the things
That fill my heart with joy
Could I make someone happy
A small girl or a boy.

I feel as young as they
Listening to their chatter
And if there be problems
I ask, what is the matter.

Why not show someone you care
Help them in what they do
By keeping busy you might find
No fear will follow you.

WAITING

You have my love and always will
And one thing I must say
There isn't time to feel regret
Since you came my way.

Remember darling all my days
Are lived for you alone
I shall be here waiting
Please call when you get home.

THE DAY

We all shed a tear
When feeling fear
Over and over again
Then came the day
Laughter held sway
Happiness grew from pain.

Tears come from sadness
Also from gladness
Be true to yourself
Why show regret
If you have been kind
Keep in mind
There is no reason
To fret.

TO JOE

Hear the heartbeat of your loved one
Being held so very close
It is true we each have heartache
Sometimes a double dose.

I shall remember darling
When you have a dreary day
Try and make you smile a little
To chase your cares away.

Just pretend you're on a sailboat
Gliding gently through the breeze
Helping someone feel less lonely
Doing this you tried to please.

BE MINE

Please listen to my heartbeat
Its telling you be mine
Seems forever to keep repeating
Sounding out three-quarter time.

Take a few short minutes
Before this day has passed you by
Lend a hand to one who loves you
Never give them cause to cry.

If yesterdays came rushing back
What tomorrow might bring
Saying three small words, I love you
Will make their heart sing.

FROM ME

Pain will be forgotten
With a prayer tho quickly said
A minute the time it takes
So bow your weary head.

Remember all the people
Less fortunate than we
Now for you I'm saying
A little prayer from me.

EMOTIONS

A smile can break the barrier
Of pent up emotions
Ease anger and frustration
A frown can cause wrinkles
That furrow you brow
And last for a long duration.

BEGINNING

If you feel tomorrow holds the answer
What happened to your promise of yesterday
Is today the new beginning
To keep from sinning
And make problems go away.

WISH

Were I able to compose a song
About the stars the sun or sea
Just like clouds on the horizon
All a mystery to me,

Should my life's span reach a hundred
With you I am satisfied
My problems were out-numbered
Faith and love were on my side.

SUMMER SUN

There was loneliness I knew
'Til the day that I met you.
Like the summer sun you took my cares away
Please stay by my side when I am your bride
The summer sun will brighten everyday.

Feeling weary and so blue
Wondering if by chance you knew
I was wishing you would turn, look at me
Like the summer sun your smile
Shone to make each day worthwhile
Sunny days find a heart so free.

Hear me begging summer sun
Keep my blues on the run
Never from me run and hide
Without the summer sun
I will be the lonely one
Never be a blushing bride.

ALONG THE WAY

Its just great seeing someone smile
Even on a cloudy day
Listen to children singing
As they go along their way.

See flower buds burst into blossom
Gloom not for lovely things
Show tenderness to someone
Harsh words only sting.

We need the rain of springtime
It helps things to grow
If the day is dark and dreary
Spread sunshine as you go.

LONESOME

Still thinking about you always will
Trying my best to understand
Why you went away so suddenly
When needing a helping hand

Hoping you reach a goal
Look for a better life
Remember somewhere along the way
You had a beautiful wife.

RAINDROP

One raindrop from a darkened sky
Won't settle any dust
Yet when the stars shine brightly
Could light the path
Of a wanderers trust.

One minute out of a lifetime
Could bring joy to someone in pain
Teach, help each other
There is much to gain.

When raindrops settle the dust
The sun comes shining through
A friend is needed, look
God who is ever true.

DID YOU KNOW

Saying you are sorry is helpful
Showing you care eases the burden.

HUMANS

Never forget I love you, wishing to see you again
Look at tomorrow; there is much we gain
If a mistake was made, God gives powerful love
Weak are we humans, seeking help from above.

WATCHFUL

Swiftly night came, being alone
Small wonder solitude
Might cause man to roam.
We must look, reach out, not be afraid
Hold to life's plan
Never regret sacrificing
Offering your hand.
Someone watches, always sees
Changes nights to days
Made the moon and stars
Why should I feel lonely
In this world of ours.
He is watchful over all
Each day through sorrow
Ask his help He listens
Today, tonight, tomorrow.

VOWS

Whisper gently you love me
Because I really care
Gently whisper as the raindrops
Cool the hot and sultry air.

When we awaken to a new day
Pledge our love anew
Then twilight sends the darkness
Only one I want is you.

Too soon it dawns tomorrow
Winds blow softly though the trees
Loving has made life beautiful
Dearest may I always please.

Evening comes and things are quiet
Our promise till the end of time
Was forever love and cherish
Keeping vows has turned out fine.

FORGIVE

Forgive the sighs of yesterday
Get going pain and sorrow
Forget times I made you cry
Laugh with me tomorrow.

AMEN

Remember to be gracious
Give no reason to offend
A bouquet, shout what life's about
Faith to the last amen.

A mile the distance you travel
Smiling goes a long, long way
With zest for every season
A prayer said each day.

Memories of love, life will not fade
Store them on the shelf
Time passes quickly for everyone
Never for each one's self.

Do not be lonely, you are not
The only one left alone
Many tears shed with prayers said
Seemed days sun never shown.

Think of years we enjoyed
With family, friends by the score
Years we had were wonderful
I must not cry any more.

Harvest a bouquet of happiness
Impossible without friends
Think of caring, doing
Giving, making amends.

FOR TED

Ted Donavan is building a replica
Of a place I used to roam
Where I lived as a child
A mere half block from my home.

Ted has the knowledge
As a designer with a rule
This place I write about
The olden, golden Yatesville school.

Located in the middle of no where
Many learned their A, B, C's
We grasped the world of wonder
So teacher and parents we could please.

Standing amid corn fields
That stood ten feet high
Each had corn bouquets at Halloween
To toss at ghosts when they passed by.

I feel Ted will do his very best
His sister Dolores told me so
When she married my brother Tom
His happiness seemed to overflow.

Ted I'm making this wish, not demand
I would like a copy for myself
Will display it proudly
Upon my great room shelf.

And if ever you visit
Down our Florida way
Bring Sis and Jim along
You're welcome any day.

DREAM WITH ME

Come dream with me a little while
In quiet awesome wonder
Freedom rings in this land of ours
Loud as the blast of thunder.

Dream with me both old and young
Let's not live the past
Grasp every precious moment
Until the very last.

Often we reach too far
A lovely thought to hold
Dreaming a gift to cherish
Especially when growing old.

So youth may all your dreams be sweet
Your lives so blessed and complete
When problems arise to cause you sadness
May those times reveal gladness.

Enjoy each day, stand tall and free
Share smiles in miles you travel
Let nothing stand in the way
Unravel difficulty into happiness each day.

HELP

Small and tiny little whispers
Uttered by a lonely child
Seeking help from dad and mother
Gives one cause to smile.

MY MIRROR

It said to me, you're getting fat
My reply I can't stand that
Realizing clothes don't fit
Seems I should take some time
Sit down and give myself a talk
Get outside, go for a walk
I hope it's just imagination
There's fat enough to feed a nation
Lent is here, it's time to try
Let no foolishness get by
Eating candy, cookies, golly gee
Not that I really want to be
Slender as a willow tree
But wintertime is no excuse
To give my body such abuse
So mirror I will start today
Shaping up and stay that way.

AFTER

When people argue and complain
Hurt lingers long after
You and me better smile
Turn bad times into laughter.

A WISH

Happiness is something we hope can someday be fulfilled.

WHISPER

Whisper gently that you love me
Because you know I really care
Quietly whisper as the raindrops
Cool the hot and sultry air.

Each day dawn awakens
To the love I feel for you
When the evening comes remember
Whisper softly darling do.

A little whisper each tomorrow
The wind blowing through the trees
Tells me life is worth living
When you try to please.

We whispered to each other
Promised till the end of time
To forever love and cherish
Keeping vows made life sublime.

Darling will you always whisper
Our years go swiftly by
Even though our hair has silvered
You seldom gave me cause to sigh.

THIRTY-TWO

Falling in love one warm spring day
In the year of thirty-two
Everyone seemed to think it odd
I was much younger than you.

There were those who gossiped
Others had little to say
You being Catholic I was not
Just hoped to be some day.

Talking with people listening a lot
Taught me with a doubt
I needed instructions to learn
Many things I was curious about.

Finding easy being a scholar
Starts with the golden rule
Living, learning, loving
Something taught in every school.

Becoming a Catholic has meant a lot
The God of humanity
Forgiven me over and over
I stumbled and fell you see.

Now there is peace and contentment
I find in my heart each day
Because the greatest of blessings in life
Is being able to pray.

THE BEAUTY

Tomorrow holds the beauty
We're expected to find
We go around the bend
Take time to pray
Along the way
A hand you might extend.

Smile the pleasure
You give will measure
Up to happiness
When wearing a frown
Turn it around
Then you might achieve success.

MISS STACEY

Miss Stacey VanderHeiden
Lives next door to me
So very small when they moved in
Now lovely as can be.

She has a pet, "Tigger" the cat
Gray and striped and very fat
Chases birds from my balcony
I certainly do like that.

Seldom I see her during school
But when summer comes, she'll have fun
Enjoying my backyard swimming pool
Spending leisure time in the warm sun.

CONCERN

Sure it hurt when you said goodbye
Which proved only too true
You fluttered around like a butterfly
Oh irresponsible you.

Trying to help in every way
When you seemed so very sad
Without a thought you turned away
Really was too bad.

Will I stay alone I cannot say
Waiting for your return
Have your fling, you silly thing
I will not show concern.

GENEROUS DEED

Wandering the path of thoughtfulness
Seeking perhaps to find
Contentment and happiness
Genuine peace of mind.

It cannot be bought
For any amount
No matter the effort
Or how high the count.

DO THIS

Never feel no one cares
Everyone is busy in their own way
Trying to improve life
Takes part of every day.

Reaching out and searching
Looking forward to time
Hoping for contentment
All things work out fine.

Spend more time enjoying life
A reason to aim higher
Each one anticipating
The day they can retire.

New ideas we think about
Are great we must agree
There is nothing wrong in dreaming
Something that is free.

WHEN

When doing for someone
Should I succeed
Happiness will follow
My generous deed.

DID YOU KNOW

Whispering a sweet nothing
Is more profitable than a rash of ugly words.

EMPTY DREAMS

Darling would you marry me
If only I ask
Wanting you to love me
Seems to have been a task.

You don't know or realize
On a day in September
Putting your arms around me
I wish you would remember.

Sometime I will tell you
Exactly how I feel
Just talking to you quietly
Makes my senses reel.

Perhaps tomorrow be the day
I ask you for a date
Just to dinner or a show
Make the day end great.

If you say no, I will understand
You are busy as can be
Always doing for someone else
This service is free.

I think you are someone special
Not part of a scheme
Loving you would be beautiful
Do I follow an empty dream.

BOOTS

Those crazy boots you gave me
Are hurting my feet so
I will try to wear them
Everywhere I go.

Sure they give me pleasure
A little pain I might say
Still promising to wear them
When you brought them home that day.

Looking around the countryside
I tried to realize
What life would be without you
Like the stars without the skies.

Come on let's do some foolish things
Be happy and carefree
I will wear those crazy boots
You had made for me.

NONSENSE

When is the time to whisper
Sweet nonsense to someone you love
With the summer breeze
Doing as you please.
Or when stars are shining above
This is the time to remember
Living really great
Share knowledge you gain
Like a golden refrain
Enjoy things before it's too late.

SECRET

I don't mind gray skies
Or any other hue
Wishing just to get along
Really this is true.

So what if we act foolish
Sometimes get to feeling blue
Just want to tell you
I'm bad when I'm with you.

When two people fall in love
Saying you're the only and only
There will be better times ahead
No more feeling lonely.

Come and visit I will tell
All my secret wishes
If I cook, you stay around
And we'll do the dishes.

Never let the lonesome bug
Get you down and out
Pick up the phone and call
Relieve your mind of doubt.

I will try to show
My love for you is true
Then I hope you realize
I'm only bad with you.

IF

If in doubt forget it
If not, you might regret it.

NO PLAN

I love to call on the phone
To hear you say hello
Seems it's been ages
Even if a few hours ago.

Uttering little secrets
Repeating small talk I might hear
Sort of flimsy excuses
Like to feel you are near.

Saying I love you softly
Something I did not plan
Then it seemed so very right
You were a lonely man.

Shall we put away all heartaches
Shove away the angry thoughts
Open the gates go happiness
Enjoy our friendly talks.

JOE

I miss you darling very much
Each hour you are not here
Hold me closely in your arms
Keep me ever near.

A wonderful someone won my heart
Seems it happened too fast
But since you said, I love you
My life is complete at last.

MY DAY

No known for fame or fortune
Enjoy life my plan
Riches of each day are mine
When helping fellow man.

A smile or warm hello can ease
The burden they might carry
Having problems as some do
Perhaps then I might tarry.

I can help, please call on me
I will not turn away
Sometime I might need love
To brighten up my day.

Knowing a friend is wonderful
What more could anyone ask
Giving some pleasure will double in measure
God helps ease the task.

MY DREAM

Climb aboard my dream
We leave pain and grief behind
Like children at play, let's wander away
Seek and we shall find.
Love enough for everyone
When day is finally done
Knowing we accomplished something
Rewarding and fun.

INSPIRATION

I should get busy doing work
The start of day
Just looking out the window
See Flowers in wonderful spring
Should give me an excellent reason
Doing most anything.

Clean the cupboard, mop the flow
Makes the windows shine
Say a pray along the way
Hope things turn out fine.

Pick up paper and read while
Unemployment's causing a mess
If everyone to work could go
There really would be progress.

Take a minute out to rest
Wishing all were well
For everybody everywhere
A story I might tell.

We have a country that's the best
In all the world's creations
We should try generously
Making peace an inspiration.

LITTLE FRIEND

Today I lost a little friend
Who never talked to me
With me a few short years
He was great company.
A tiny young silver poodle
Came to make our house his home
His weight would be ten pounds at most
When being fully grown.
He sure liked getting groomed
His hair soft as tissue silk
A real blue blood was Po-Po.
Liking his cheese and milk
Always ready for a ride
Anytime night or day
Almost smart enough to talk
And understood what you say.
Up the stairs on the chairs
Chasing to and fro
When some stranger came around
He would let us know.
Parting with a little pet
Very difficult most agree
Because he had more sense than many
Who talk like you and me.

OUR TALENT

A necessity to live
Laugh and care
With quiet simplicity
Why can't we share.

Talent of loving our neighbor
Gift of energy to show
When forgiving reap a harvest
Make one's heart overflow.

EACH DAY

Wanting each day for someone
Better than those past
Giving thanks for precious years
May they forever last.

Ask forgiveness when I hurt
Someone needlessly
Never argue or find fault
That's acting foolishly.

ALWAYS

Jesus listen closely
Hear my humble prayer
The Mass has many changes
With your help I'll do my share.

Learn the modern method
Teach us Master ever wise
Believe, please don't forsake us
To you we owe our lives.

You promise blessings always
Grant pardon when we sin
Seems we are always pleading
May we be healed within.

Even though my sins are many
Will you comfort me
When begging forgiveness
My prayer on bended knee.

HAND IN HAND

Spring at last
Winter's blast
Seems to have gone away
Let's pledge anew
Our love so true
Maybe you will stay.
Watch a stream
Pin a dream
On white clouds driving by.
Listen to my heart saying
Darling won't you try.
Love me dearest
Soon we could make our plan
Walk down the aisle
Hand in hand.
It's good to know
Our love will last
Thru coming years
Then maybe tiny footsteps
Will bring joy and happy tears.

CARE

A dream can't become a reality
When unwilling to care
Just thoughts that haunt them
Nobody wants them
When they turn into a nightmare.

HAPPY SMILE

A stranger came to visit
Could not stay long you see
He was on the way to somewhere
I ask, where might this be.

Maybe a warmer climate
Just to feel the ocean breeze
We told him that happiness
Could offer most of these.

He said you have family
Loved ones, mine have forgotten me
Being sad we were glad
To have his company.

Easing pain we ask quickly
Could you stay a little while
'twas like the door to heaven opened
His response a happy smile.

LITTLE ELF

Do not let a worry bother
Act like a little elf
Chase away with smile so tender
Each owes this to himself.

MANKIND

Burdens of this world
Seems would cause God to despair
Yet he reaches out his arms
Willingly to care.

The chance asking forgiveness
Each and everyone alive
Knowing too well without him
Mankind cannot survive.

WHY

You filled me days with happiness
Then left me wondering why
Leaving so suddenly
Even failed to say goodbye.

If you wish not to remember
I won't feel regret
Looking ahead to better things
It is God you must not forget.

THE FLOWER

The fragrance of the flower
Faded when you said goodbye
I shall pick one to replace it
Hoping tears will quickly dry.

HOLIDAY HAPPINESS

Hear the sounds of Christmas
Laughter of children at play
Around the world everyone's thinking
Someone special is coming our way.

Looking at the beauty
Decorations and gifts to grand
Matter not six or sixty
Christmas is for every man.

Tis a merry time I wish for all
Whenever you pass my way
With happiness in it, let's share a minute
Helping somebody enjoy their day.

Listen, sounds of the holiday
Filled with fun and pleasure
Choirs sing and church bells ring
Leaving memories to treasure.

Share the goodness of Christmas
With family, relatives and friends
Think of the mile in every smile
That peace on earth extends.

With love in your heart at Christmas
Join in laughter and mirth
A common bond holds us together
Glorious time of the savior's birth.

WHAT'S THE USE

Pray for people of all nations
Live by faith and not the sword
Teach the love of God forever
Believe his almighty word.
If you fall along the wayside
Arise. Carry on your share
Because you know life is eternal
Have courage don't despair.
At times face temptation
Sadly thinking what's the use
Could we have stood his agony
Or ever find excuse.
To church you did not go
Are you tired, only selfish
Thinking who will ever know.
There is only one Creator
Died for all humanity
If each nation pulled together
We would live in harmony.
Silent as the sea at ebb tide
Give yourself a chance to call
When you are troubled
Although busy, He has time for all.

GOOD MORNING

Looking out the window
At starting of day
Eastern sky glowing
My mind far away.

Just being happy
Healthy and wise
Is really a treasure.
I do realize.

Today I must try
Bring some joy
Sharing and caring
Present a toy.

To a small friend
Or gift for a shut-in
Not waste a minute
Let my day begin.

From the time the sun rises
Till its going down
Wondering what can bring
Smiles instead of frown

Chase away tears
Not meant to be
Making my day worthwhile
Giving pleasure for me.

TIME TO FORGIVE

Never doubt almighty God
He knows what is best
For all of creation
Puts them to the test

I found myself wondering why
They felt that he must die
Cause to shudder everyone
That placed the cross
From which he hung.

Have faith people one and all
Show your belief in God
Time to forgive much too late
When laid beneath the sod.

Try doing, loving, giving
No matter what you say
If only just a daily prayer
Make a brighter day.

We thank each day for giving
Freedom without restriction
Work and worship as we please
A great benediction.

Our land of peace for everyone
Love of family and friends
Tomorrow be willing to share
It's what God intends.

A NEW DAY

My heart skips a beat
Awakening to a new day
Knowing that tomorrow
Will being happy thoughts my way.

Stay close beside me
Open your arms
Seeing you smile gives a thrill
We share a future
With blessings and good will.

Remember the past
Live in the present
Take each day in stride
Unhappy memories will fade
A new day on our side.

Charity means doing for others
At home and mission fields afar
Little candle at the altar
Shine like evening star.

Tiny candle may your flame
Be a silent prayer from me
Help somewhere a lonesome sinner
Find forgiveness and serenity.

PLEASE RETURN

A blade of grass a single rosebud
Leaves blowing in the gentle wind
My heart beats with tender longing
Waiting for a loving friend.

Footsteps on the stairway
Tell me you are home
We will spend the night together
Then tomorrow you will roam.

Try to share pain and sorrow
Grief someone must bear
Give hope and understanding
Showing graciously you care.

Offer prayers for all in trouble
Asking them to please return
Be forgiving and forgetting
Helping them is your concern.

Happiness is remembering today
You helped someone along the way
Willing to walk and extra mile
Love gave you a smile.

Thinking one thing. Doing another
Help an unfortunate brother
Carrying his cross you earn a reward
Life everlasting, the Master's word.

A CHANCE

We know with eyes to see
And hands to touch
Given legs to walk around
A chance to pray, live another day
See happiness abound.

WALK A MILE

Why must there be suffering
I would rather walk a mile
To ease the pain of someone
Just to see them smile.

Offer a hand, reach out
Share some joy and laughter
Make their world shine again
Good deeds what we're after.

MAGIC

Did you ever watch the sunset
Turn the evening sky to gold
All too soon the night appears
Then a mystery could unfold.

The moon in glorious splendor rises
Magic we don't understand
We take much for granted
With the wonders in this land.

We need the oceans, mountains, and deserts
Along with fertile soil
The magic of the harvest
Worth the work and toil'

Then after night the dawn awakens
Like magic to living things
Each in curious anticipation
Wonder what the new day brings.

REFLECTIONS

Kneeling in church silently
Sun of the day is going down
Stained glass windows give reflections
The Lord's presence all around.

Altars stand in majesty
To speak they might say
Today I have been slighted
Very few stopped to pray.

Have we gone modern in religion
There are changes ever new
Teach us better understanding
Our faith we know is true.

I feel that I am sharing
Silence at a loss
Help to bear the burden
Of the heavy wooden cross.

Our sins are still forgiven
Just as they were before
God heard prayers same as always
He will never close the door.

Perhaps you are unhapps
About prayers said, songs sung
Who would take His place
On the cross where He hung.

TOUCH SOMEONE

Might I reach out in happiness
Touch someone with my love
Thanking all the saints in heaven
Watching o'er me with love.

A WISH

To everyone no matter where
A wish, the very best you see
Go about this day and always
Doing your most, happy be.

OTHERS

May I always be worthy
Asking help for others
Peace and understanding
All might live as brothers.

Be a neighbor to everyone
Kind to those we love
Doing deeds for someone's need
With guidance from above.

SO TIRED

On my knees weeding the flower bed
Beginning to feel tired
When you pause to say hello
I became inspired, worked a bit faster
Willing to get done
Then relaxed in the pool
Enchanted by the sun.

PAIN AND STRESS

When looking if pain I show
May it not bother you
Each person is entitled
Having a fault or two

I know living is pleasure
Having enjoyed happiness
Remembering it's not this world
That causes pain and stress.

People you meet each day
With problems to relate
Needing someone to confide in
Not listening would create.

A feeling of resentment
Are you good for spending time
Share a laugh or two
Show you can be kind.

When pain I show, be patient
Please forgive me times I frown
None of us should ever feel
Walls are tumbling down.

A smile oft times hides heartache
Weariness they might show
Try looking at their side of life
Let understanding grow.

THE THRONG

Smile while you pass along
The highway known as life
Many happy joyful days
O'er come the times of strife.

If alone you are lonesome
Look out the window to see
Golden beauty to last forever
No cost, it's all free.

Each have a chance doing better
Lives filled with song
Be a real go-getter
Its magic being one of the throng.

Be known for fun and laughter
What more could anyone ask
God's on our side to guide
Fulfillment of life no task.

LITTLE TIME

Greetings are a real joy
Just as living a pleasure
Offering a helping hand
Gives hope beyond all measure.

Take time it matters
Be a very special friend
Success is found in doing
Leaves no reason to pretend.

RETURN

As whispering winds
Sifting sands
And oceans roar
I hear you calling
Please come home
And roam no more.
Patiently I wait for you
Breathe a sigh
Spring has come my darling
Return to me
Then I can thank the
Sifting sands and ocean breeze
Being alone is like
A home without a lullaby.
When doubt you feel
I will reveal tenderness
Come back and bring
Peace, happiness
Thanks to the wind
The ocean roar
They heard my plea
With your caress
I have been blessed
You're home with me.

HOLD MY HAND

What is living without love
Each needs someone to care
You are alone so am I
Let's get together and share
Dinner, show or sit and talk
Could be enjoyment and fun
Sitting beside me, holding my hand
Blues are on the run.

In secret I will call you Joey
Have for a long time
Next time I see you I might say
I love you, will you be mine.
Sitting along by the phone
Why not call just to say Hi
Wanting you near always
To me you're quite a guy.

IDLE

Idle hours people talk about
Are not for me
With time so freely given
What can the problem be.
Lift the load of someone weary
Whether morn or set of sun
Enjoy each day that's given
Fill idle hours with fun.

WESTERN SONGS

Now I don't sing grand opera
Or croon like Mr. Bing
Not fond of Rock & Roll
But songs with a western swing.

The old prairie was lonesome
Not much fun around
When coyotes are howling
They leave an eerie sound.

When round-up time is over
The branding is all done
Come on grab that old guitar
Let western songs be sung.

The cowboys sure laugh at me
I get tougher every day
Aches and pains I soon forget
When western tunes they play.

Now I abandoned city life
Like a puppet on a string
Contentment fills my heart each time
Those cowboys start to sing.

Whether it's a yodel
About some lonely lad
Time I spent out west
The best I've ever had.

HE HEARS US

Humbly we kneel, bow our heads
To worship him
Ask his blessings
Then say amen.

Each hour we live
Each day goes by
Need him now and when we die
He hears us.

Mary his mother hears our plea
We pray for humanity
All may live a better life
Not interfere in time of strife.

Remembering each time
We pray
We will begin to live his way
He hears us.

DAYS END

A good days beginning, a happy days end
Mixed with some prayer, a pleasure my friend.

DAYDREAMING

If it weren't for you
where would I be
Alone and lonesome
Perhaps couldn't see
Dawn of a new day
Bright sunny hours
Spent daydreaming
Waiting for showers.
The earth is dry
Wind blows free
When vacation is over
Please come home to me.
If not for you
I would spend lonely hours
Wondering what you are doing
In this great land of ours.
I will be happy
On your return
Don't think me foolish
Showing concern.
My love is forever
This will not change
Seems like a miracle
Let's not rearrange
Keep me in your thoughts
My life is worth living
If ever I hurt
Will you be forgiving.

ALWAYS A SUN

Saying I love you not foolish
Never playing a part
Nor any game to me
When offering my heart.

Forever a long, long time
That is how a river flows
Sometimes shallow, sometimes deep
The way my love for you grows.

Forever I will love you
Like the river that runs
Gaining momentum at every turn
There will always be a sun.

Kissing me on St. Patrick's Day
The first time in your life
Though only lasting a second
It seemed very right.

Part of acting foolish
Keep hoping you really care
Willing to help when troubled
Trying to do my share

Thanks for the way you smiled
When we met crossing the street
You added depth to the meaning
Of life, because you were sweet.

SPECIAL ONE

Everything has a beginning
Life, work, day and night
There is beauty believing
When doing a thing with might.

The love of man for woman
The handclasp of a friend
Sharing of a secret
At the journeys end.

I found a new beginning
You stopped to say hello
It blossomed into loving
Seems days just overflow.

When a feeling of belonging
To a special one
The starting of new life
Bright as morning sun.

TRY

If a problem we share
A wrong, let's make it right
Never close the door on anger
Try with all your might.

Hold each other very close
With a tender embrace
Love we give each other
In keeping with God's grace.

PETALS

Something that shows in a garden
Can also be found on a hill
A gift for all even strangers
Known to each God's will.

Reach out when there are problems
Why waste another day
Ask for help, you will find
Nothing stands in the way.

Life, love, laughter, happiness
May be found in a very small space
Pick a few petals for living
From the bouquet filled with grace.

Never turn from forgiveness
Though pain, wear smiles on your face
Come on mankind remember
We are the human race.

What if colors are different
Life's ambition we hope to fill
Stand straight and tall as the willow
Drink from the fountain of good will.

Faith a stranger to many
Hope a promise to all
May each be blessed for knowledge
A gift I often recall.

A POEM

This short poem that I write
Has meaning without end
Because a stranger stopped, asked
Will you be my friend.

THE PATHWAY

If I try willingly
To lend a helping hand
You might know some pleasure
Perhaps even understand.

Living can be beautiful
The pathway easy we trod
Loving, caring, sharing
With the help of God.

Letting despair and loneliness
Follow wherever you go
The road to peaceful living
Won't be easy I know.

Others have known heartache
This road you travel alone
Still they found happiness
By good deeds they have sown.

THE THORN

The thorn of a rose is a sticky thing
A peculiar person, a picky thing.

SUNSHINE

Reaching out you took my hand
Whispered of your love
On bended knee I'm asking
Worthy of gifts from above.

Our paths never crossed before
Though I waited patiently
Seems after a lifetime
There you were for me.

Please may I bring sunshine
My promise to you this day
Good fortune finds me
Because you showed the way.

Thanks to faith in listening
Quiet like the call of a dove
There are family and wonderful friends
And you to share my love.

FOREVER

Please don't go away
Will you stay
Be part of my life.
When you are near
There is no fear, nor care
My open arms will hold you close
Helping your pain to share.

WHO GIVES A DARN

A day for love and laughter
The world seems upside down
Things go on a long time after
We are placed beneath the ground.

Gripe, complain, walk with bent shoulders
No one gives a darn
Wear a smile, bear your burden
Add to your health and charm.

Linger o'er the golden moments
Think of loved ones far away
Each and everyone has problems
Wishing for a better day.

Write a post card, send a letter
Or extended telephone call
It will be appreciated
Winter, summer spring and fall.

STARS IN MY EYES

Love you darling, do you realize
You make the stars light up my eyes
Cause me to laugh, never frown
Be my sweetheart, I'll not let you down.

WISHING

Wishing today for happiness
Making the most of my years
Tomorrow will come like the rising sun
Drive away my tears.

TO LIVE WITH MAN

We raise our voices giving praise
Acknowledge best we can
Religious faith no matter which
We need to live with man.

Everyone has their fault
Peace of mind comes from
What we do
One cannot live alone my friend
Proven to be true.

Leave to believe not deceive
When someone wants to know
Do you think there is a God
Why does mankind suffer so.

Religious leaders of all faith
Struggling to guide
Sing aloud, show them you're proud
To walk side by side.

I feel if all humbly pray
Hear our voices Lord
A united Christian country
Could live without the sword.

Yes there is a God my friend
Ask his help each day
Please don't forsake your children
Grant our wish, another day.

ALL MEN

We live to see the day when
All men will be free again
The nations gather
Knowledge from each other
Walk side by side unified
Calling each one brother.

Could we reach out a helping hand
Promising to understand
The path that all trod
Everyone in faith someday
Willingly will kneel and pray
For their belief in God.

FRIENDSHIP

On reaching out to grasp your hand
A brilliant smile broke through
You moved here from far away
That's when our friendship grew.

Now it's goodbye, no regrets
Just reach out once again
God will help when I ask
Sometime to love again.

YOUR WILL

Only your will be done a task
You cannot do things alone
Asking each day to worthy be
Leaves little reason to moan.
Promises we're always making
Many times failing to keep
Forgive a penitent sinner
Who has been careless and weak.

SATISFIED

Down through the years
I have know fears
Pain and sadness pushed aside
Now hoping someday you look my way
I will be satisfied

Never darling to hurt you
May we forget the past
Open your arms hold me
Love is sure to last

Life is beautiful together
Leaving makes me sad
Call on the phone when lonely
Then my heart will be glad.

TREASURES

Life is not yours alone
Grasp a forgotten one
Might be included
Is that too much to ask
Not yours alone to judge
Their faults at beginning or end
Get involved be concerned
Show you are a friend.

You left, seems without a care
Pain its given me
Never trying to live your life
Just helped when needed be.

Take care, be good, go to church
Learn your manners well
Friends you meet, write me about
There should be much to tell.

Don't seek the road to easy street
Willingly do your share
If you store up treasures
God will keep you in His care.

OUR SALVATION

In church we sing, a holy thing
About God and creation
Praise him adoringly, he is our salvation
When we feel all is lost
Our focus should be
Father, son and spirit, blessed trinity.

Seems the savior of mankind
Hung upon the cross
Died for sins of many
What a bitter loss.

Three days passed, he arose
Triumphant into heaven
And in his goodness
Sins are forgiven

Modern world, modern times
Let our voices ring
Praise the almighty
Our salvation, our king.

DREAMERS

The time of year makes
Dreamers of children
This I know
School is out
Then July four
Summer is here
Joys overflow
Vacations start for many
Traveling far and wide
Swimming, tennis, biking
Keeps them occupied
Too soon it's September
Back to school again
Meeting new friends
Playing football
Now the leaves of Fall
Then Halloween
At October's end
Here we are in November
Turkey time not far away
Its joy has two meanings
Thanksgiving and a holiday
Then the greatest of them all
Here comes good December
Expected gifts, happy times
Pleasures to remember
Jesus' birthday, Santa Claus
Snow, frostbite sting
Wishing a Merry Christmas
To everyone
Hearing church bells ring.

YESTERDAYS, TOMORROWS, FOREVER

Yesterdays, tomorrows, forever
I've loved you all this time
Wanting you close beside me
Looking back on life sublime.

There is always forgiveness
Just hold out your arms
Loving you never secret
Nor tiring of your charms

Don't throw away memories
Keep them locked in your heart
Always something to cherish
Playing an important part.

There will be lovers forever
Have been through the ages of time
Someone to love a treasure
Having you near is divine.

The yesterdays and the tomorrows
The forever we live each day
Are storing up miles of pleasure
As we travel life's way.

When each day dawns remember
A wish for everyone love
How precious are the moments
And blessings from above.

BE TRUE

We all shed a tear
When feeling fear
Over and over again
Then comes the day
Happiness held sway
Laughter grew from pain.

Tears come from gladness
Or sadness or regret
Just be true to yourself
Remembering, time spent together
Whether in good and bad weather
Something you won't forget

AGE

So when your eyes
Grow dim my love
Please don't wear a frown
I open my arms
Hold you close
Never let you down.
Age makes no difference
When two people care
Sharing a beautiful love
Many searched but never found
Faith like ours from above.

OUR JACK

I miss the best pal I ever had
The greatest pet, bar none
He came to us, thanks Judy
We gave Jack a good home.

Jack understood each thing said
Our eyes are filled with tears
Yet the pain he suffered
Beyond our imaginary fears.

I talked to Jack like he was human
The eight years, what a joy
Left us many memories
Like a child with a toy.

Jack loved riding in the car
Whenever we'd say "go"
He would run to the door and wait
As if putting on a show.

Goodbye Dear Jack I will cry
Tears stain my face
My memories long will linger
No other will take your place.

Joan would take him for a walk
Up and down the street
He stopped to sniff each tree or shrub
Greet every neighbor he would meet.

[OUR JACK—continued]

All children loved our Jack
On their way or coming from school
He loved their attention but never jumped or barked
That against the rule.

Ernie called him "Happy Jack"
He and Margot live on the corner
Jack knew each and every driveway
As if he were the owner.

Don and I miss our Jack
The best friend we ever had
Leaving us on 4-24-05
No dog will ever take his place
He made life great; good to be alive.

Casey and Sandy had a pet
They lost Pepper a few months ago
So they know what we suffer
Our hearts the pain does grow.

Jack's death came suddenly
We lost our buddy, pal and friend
May he be playful in dog heaven
Be a friend to Polo and Joe.

What it means losing a pet
Memories difficult to forget
Tears shed to overflow
Leaves heartache long and slow.

[OUR JACK—continued]

Jack we miss you, always will
Life is hard losing a friend
Greeting each who come to visit
When will the pain end?

There are so many memories
Of our precious little boy
Our hearts are filled with sadness
We lost our cause for joy.

You really did understand everything
You could do everything but talk
You provided Don cause for daily exercise
Let him know when you wanted to take a walk.

In the early mornings when we came in
Don would say, just a minute and you'd sit
Until he'd dry your little paws
Dew made them wet.

Don would tell you, I love you Jack
You'd then kiss him on the nose
We miss our loving, intelligent Schnauzer
How much, only God knows.

We have a beautiful silk flower
Received from Joan and Charlie that day
It is in heartfelt sympathy
Such a thoughtful bouquet.

[OUR JACK—continued]

Jack I say just a farewell
May you remember your friend
To me you were *human*
So I say God Bless, Amen

NEW BEGINNING

May you enjoy the very best
As you start a new beginning
Always be appreciative
Then you will be winning.

Having all the good things
Sharing them together
Should storm clouds gather
Blame them on the weather.

Talk things out, don't hesitate
Let pain not turn to sorrow
A future wished beautiful things
Fill each day tomorrow.

Reach out, look up share
Each memory to treasure
The road ahead filed with hope
Please take time to measure.

Remember the mile in everyone's smile
The day will be lighter
When looking back on yesterdays
Tomorrows will be brighter.

I THINK

Today is what yesterday was
Or would that be tomorrow
Thinking about something silly as this
Won't leave time for sorrow.

IF

If each day we look for joy
I am sure all will see
We are not forsaken
God loves us tenderly.

HELLO

Did you even think sitting alone
You might bring some gladness
Saying hello over the phone
Could chase away their sadness.

Stopping by, go for a walk
Have them for dinner tomorrow
Happiness in their voices tell you
Kindness chased away sorrow.

KEEPING WATCH

Oft times I pause and think about
Happy times I have known
Friends who understood
Kindness that was shown.
Great love for life given
Though now I walk alone
A guardian angel is keeping watch
No matter when I roam.
Being blessed to serve another day
Humbly saying a prayer
For someone lonesome just like me
Willingly I will share.
Reaching past the age of sixty eight
We are the generation
Holding up our country
With generous population.

THE STORM

Thunder and lightning started
Rain came pouring down
Washed away the dirt of winter.
Tulips, crocus and daffodils pushing up their heads.
Blossoms greet the Easter season, time to plant a flower bed.

The summer is upon us, what might humans ask
Than hear children laughing having fun, they grow up fast.
Soon they must conquer problems of turmoil known
Which besiege all people, not one individual alone.

So the storm they brought us lightning. The heavy thunder roar
Gone like the Easter season, it will soon be July 4
A different kind of celebration known as Independence
If nations gather in peace, may each be in attendance.

ERNIE

We had a very special friend
Living up at number two
Foxfords Chase the address
It is tough to bid adieu.

Being a neighbor tried and true
Enjoying a visit in your home
You and Margot perfect hosts
Talking about places we used to roam.

Seems the years pass quickly
Do we take the time
Look back on the yesterdays
While remembering life was mighty fine.

The yesterdays gone forever
Tomorrows never come
I know Ernie's Guardian Angel
Was there to lead him home.

Don and I miss you Ernie
May you enjoy peace and rest
God called, you answered
You were one of his best.

God bless and keep you Ernie
Each day I implore
The gate of heaven opened
When you knocked on the door.

THANK YOU TOPEKANS
Written June 1964

I attended the district meeting of the ABWA*
Held in Topeka, Kansas on the first thru third of May
The chapter chosen to be host should really be commended
Set a district record on the numbers who attended.

The Jayhawk was so crowded, Howard Johnson's was our host
Our suite of rooms I'll say really were the most
We saw so many things as we motored all around
To and from convention headquarters in the heart of town.

The boodle bags they gave us filled with odds and ends rare
Proved that each and every member had to do her share
Touring all around the city planned so well and really great
Our guide, Frances Smith, works for this sovereign state.

We saw Topeka High School a red brick institution
The flag pole mounted on the lawn a part from the ship "Constitution"
Gage Park where people enjoy life, much for one to see
And the mansion of your governor in rolling green country.

"Menninger Foundation" is known both far and wide
Speakers told about their work, one acted as a guide
Time had come to see more sights, Landon's home came into view
hospitals, churches, schools, lovely homes, and the sky so blue.

The State Fairgrounds are silent now as in hibernation
Halls of the capitol are showing, "Art of a native son creation."
The grandeur of a million sights, the State Office Building the best
The Santa Fe, can proudly say they serve the great Midwest.

[THANK YOU TOPEKANS—continued]

Back to the Jayhawk once again, tired oh boy I'll say
That trip was great you really rate planning such a day
Here's to Topeka Chapter, may be offer up a toast
Come visit us in Springfield, we'd like to be your host.

Now to business, for workshops, bulletins, scrapbooks large or small
The judges had a problem looking at them all
Remember please the organist, her playing was just grand
About 500 chatting women she had a job on hand.

The vocalists were good, sang with inspiration
Here's hoping they will go far seeking their vocation
Noted speakers one and all, their messages did bring
Each chapter knew, their job to do before another spring.

Last not least by far, great actor of the day
As happy as a Leprechaun, Butch O'Malley had his say—
Here's to Lucille, hope you feel our deep appreciation
Bringing joy to many people, helps make a better nation
So lend an ear and listen here, this statement I will make
Someday I'll visit once again your great Midwestern state.

*American Business Women's Association

CHICAGO, OUR TOWN

The city where magic can always be found
Its fabulous lake brings joy year 'round
Skyscraper buildings, the theatres, sights
And Michigan Avenue with all its lights.

There's fun to be had, life to enjoy
Education and glamour for each girl and boy
There'll be laughter and sadness or maybe a frown
Still we love Chicago, our kind of town.

We like the big city, we're small town you see
But Chicago is our town, gay and carefree
There's baseball and football and other sports
We laugh with our neighbors as each one reports.

It seems like a million folks work in this town
In offices, banks and stores of renown.
The subways, the El's, the wide city streets
Offer people who visit a day full of treats.

There is O'Hare Field a place that's the most
Hop on a jet lines and fly coast to coast
We hope you don't mind, is loudly we boast
How gracious Chicago our town was a host.

VIEW ON CRESTVIEW

Arising in the morning
Like a vision in your dreams
Amid quiet and peaceful surroundings
Day dawns on hillside and stream.

See the sunrise over Crestview Drive
Dew from the lawn disappear
Fill your heart with gladness everyone
Leave no place for sadness or fear.

OUR RICK

A lad with such a zest for life
Keeps me on the run
Not quiet for a minute
From start of day to set of sun.

Over night he wants to stay
Home is just so far away
Then comes next morn clear and bright
Hey, can I stay again tonight.

First outside then come in
Grandma can I eat again
Get lonesome, how could this be
When grandson Rick stays with me.

HURRICANE CHARLEY

Charley was a hurricane
Shook our state with force
Destruction everywhere one looked
On a widespread course.

Danger came at 6:15
Friday, August 13, 2004
We had trees uprooted
Pool screen damaged more.

Taken lives of many people
Homes number by the score
Churches, schools and condos
A thousand trees or more.

Men came from many places
We had no power, no phones
Many suffered the loss
Critical for hospitals, nursing homes.

Workers did their very best
To clear the streets, restore power
Patience needed to suffice
There was danger every hour.

Brave men giving us their all
Many hours of every day
We had curious families
Drive around in sheer dismay.

[HURRICANE CHARLEY—continued]

Me, I'm not nosey
To view misfortunes of anyone
I stayed at home, said a prayer
Saying thanks for a job well done.

Volunteers came from many miles
Just like for the fires in nineteen ninety-eight
We left our home for five long days
Came back to celebrate.

View the loss we suffered
We could fix up after while
With all the devastation
Mary's statue seemed to greet us with a smile.

A message for help to all in need
Anytime in their life
Say a prayer for all who suffered
On this earth of war and strife.

Yes we needed help from others
As nerves began to crack
Had our men in uniform been home
Instead of deployment to Iraq.

MAUREEN, GREG, TOM, ALEXA, TERRY, MISSY

Come and visit anytime
Away from winter's cold
We entertain with ease
As gently blows the breeze.

Welcome mat at the door
Will open wide
Greeting those who enter
With love, friendship and pride.

No freezing weather from the north
Leave that stuff at home
Put away your shovels
The beach is where we roam.

No scooping snow or blustering wind
Nor salt for icy streets
Or goulashes over your shoes
No heavy blankets over sheets.

You won't need heavy extra clothes
Nor woolen socks to warm your toes
Chapped cheeks, ear muffs, gloves
We wonder here, "What are those?"

Come on down to the sunshine state
Drink Manhattans, stay up late
Do what we please, shop as we choose
Years go by, what have we to lose.

CHRISTMAS 2004

What Christmas means to me
Love, hope family or friend
Cards, letters addressing
Sending a blessing
A prayer ending with Amen.
Come and go to many places
May each say Peace
Add a few lines to someone lonely
May be a father, mother, sister, brother
Or could be the one and only.
Remember the season with proper reason
Regardless of any kind of weather
With warmth in your heart
You can be a part
Offer peace when praying together.
If you hold out your hand
I am sure it will blend
When all say a prayer
Lift your voice in song
You will feel you belong
As you travel most anywhere.

A PRAYER

God grant the courage to forgive
The one who made the call
Starting a war from freedom land
That brought pain to all.

Grant us peace and understanding
As we mourn tears are shed
We wonder asking why
This answer remains unsaid.

Being born in one nine one four
Having witnessed countless faces
Of our troops going off to fight
In many foreign places

Hoping the prayers of many
Might help each understand
The leaders in Washington
Each life taken, their command.

TERROR

On September eleven year 2001
At the time when New York was starting to hum
People going to work happy and free
Why terrorists ... a mystery to me.

We Americans love our country stand by its side
Work for a living do with pride
Opened our borders for all to abide
Had no fear, nothing to hide.

Trusted our leaders protecting the land
Overlooking enemies with a devious plan
Who ravished our buildings and lives in their stride
Where peace loving people work and reside.

We will not forget, long may be live
Wonder if ever we can forgive
Blessing for injured may soon all be well
And the children in happiness dwell.

We pray for the victims, tears in our eyes
Offering help when asked all who survive
God gave each an angel took them to heaven
No sin on their souls all were forgiven.
On flights 175,93, 77 and 11.

LEST WE FORGET

Neighbors, friends, from many places
Expressed feelings and regret
There were some who may say
Why he was just a pet.

He was a friend to everyone
When Don took him for a walk
Many folks have big hearts
Would stop for a moment to talk.

Joan, Bill and Jennifer, Margot, Frank and JJ
Would see Jack most every day
He understood each greeting
Patiently listening to what they might say.

Casey and Sandy, Frank and Barbara and others
Sent many cards remembering out pet
Nothing can take Jack's place
As tears of sadness are wept.

Now we have no little Jack
To greet us every morn
Waiting when we returned from Mass
Was like a dream reborn.

AGES OF PAGES VARIATION

If e'er you feel as you
Relive the ages
Just get out your memory book
Read some of the pages
They will give you pleasure
Beyond your greatest dream
Olden times remembered
Of today's what might have been
See a snapshot of yourself
Think oh no, that can't be me
When grandchildren laugh
And shout how awful, golly-gee
Clothes you wore back then now embarrass me
I tell the girls no bare mid-rifts
Or eight inch shorts to show
We were proud of how we looked
Not how much or far could we go
Back then we were proud
Not how much we could bare
Pleasing a youthful crowd
So I will look at photographs
Memory books from olden years
I will think of many times
And memories of my peers.

HEART

Your heart is the voice of happiness
Giving us peace of mind
Remembering to pause and think
Causes us to be kind.

It's wiser than the sages
We have studied in the past
So we must take care, protect
With courage to hold fast.

The mind may lead us forward
Guide both hands and feet
Aid us on the path of life
Being kind to all we meet.

When you get excited, tired
Stop and think a minute
My heart will lead me always
If I put some effort in it.

Hands, heart, mind, body,
What more can a human ask
Heart to live, mind for knowledge
When taken care of life will last.

IDEAS

Form your life with memories
As each day passes by
Jot down your ideas daily
Ponder o'er them with a sigh.

What happened yesterday
Where was I going tomorrow
Did I fail to say hello
Say a prayer for someone's sorrow.

Maybe extend a helping hand
Or thought to ease their pain
Easing the burden carried
So they could smile again.

Memories are made from simple things
Yours to treasure as time goes by
Share them with love daily
It's worthy of a try.

Blessings are for everyone
Keep on offering them or repeat
Live life to fullest measure
Shower love on all you meet.

PRAY

Dear God I offer thanks today
I have been very angry of my actions
And I pray
Receive the pain
Offer it in hope
My pain will soon be over
And I will no longer mope
Around and cause a problem
Hear my plea
Bear what my problem be
Realize many others
Are suffering more than me
So many people in this world
Have given their life
Please dear Lord I am asking
On bended knee
Take a hand where suffering
Try to set the USA free.

.... *ATIONS*

A—what causes agitation

B—because you offer beautification

C—calling for concentration

D—dealing with determination

E—easing care brings elation

F—facing life with frustration

G—going to a graduation

H—having found a sound foundation

I—imagine my imagination

J—joking about a vaccination

K—knowledge of a foreign nation

L—love will bring liberation

M—give someone motivation

N—never forget a notation

O—be aware of the operation

P—plan a trip to a plantation

Q—quiz about a quotation

R—someone's restoration

S—settle for a great sensation

T—to hear tales of tribulation

U—utilization of unification

V—did someone cause vexation

W—without causing consternation

X—expecting exhilaration

Y—yearning for motivation

Z—zoom in on moderation

WITH LOVE

Margot you are a trooper
Who bore your burden well
Unless one has lost a husband
They know not how we feel.

With memories never forgotten
Of laughter, fun and love
Between you and Ernie
Beautiful to remember, thank heaven above.

You both were wonderful neighbors
When Don and I were invited down
Pleasure like that meant much to me
More than a night on the town.

Your friendship, a blessing I hold dear
So Margot hold your memories near
Of love for Ernie every day
His star is shining up heaven's way.

WISH

My Christmas wish was offered
In a Mass of celebration
That all who strayed everywhere
Return, give thanks across our nation.

The faith of everyone I love
Shown in their own way
Christendom will last forever
When in their heart they let it stay.

I love seeing little children
Speak to the man called Santa Claus
Some have manners filled with joy
Asking for themselves and others
Please remember the girls and boys

A child said if you do not have enough
To go around, I have things at home
Please take my share
I'll wait until next Christmas
Because I know you will be there.

SERVING

Having traveled a million miles
Thousands of steps were taken
I enjoyed trips made at night
Flying in as towns awaken.

Having friends living on the mount
England is a place to see
Also some in Celle, Germany
And Catholic nuns in county Meath
At St. Joseph's convent Navan, Ireland
A place of quiet prayer and peace.

There is much to life in living
Wondrous people everywhere
I learned to speak Italian
So enjoyed myself while there.

Born in a place called Lees Summit, Missouri
July 20th, ninety years ago
The third in line of number eight
Five brothers came along after me.

Four served their country
Army, Navy, and Marines
We sent packages to them
When received, was like a dream.

THE PLAN

The sea of life holds promises
Which all should ne'er deny
Because the joy of living
As the sun shines way up high.

Ideas we had yesterday
Were mammoth in our mind
Viewing the wonders
That welcome all mankind.

Hold on to dreams of yesteryear
They bring back memories
Share happiness with someone
Help dry a falling tear.

No one likes being alone or lonely
Because time takes its toll
Share a thought of confidence
Ease one's heart and soul.

The world is full of anxiety
On the earth it was God's plan
When He created where we live
His idea not a demand.

Pray for peace, faith, love
While on this earth we trod
Brings happiness to believers
His name Almighty God.

TRAVEL

I often think about
Places I have been
Oceans crossed, mountains, deserts
When my mind travels back again.

Gaining knowledge from many countries
Visiting sights with elation
Takes me back to younger years
And wonders found in jubilation.

The British Isles were wonderful
Italy was truly grand
The alps in Switzerland
Enchanting for a country
Gives a chance to understand.

England, Ireland, Scotland, Wales
Budapest, Hungary, Germany
Places I read about when just a youth
Fulfilled my wish with ecstasy.

We have many places in the USA
Each different in their way
However foreign travel important
The educational way.

AMEN

A basket of roses
Bouquet of love
Bright sunny morning
A gray turtle dove.

Offer a smile to
Someone you meet
Either close to home
Or any street.

Hi to a child
On their way to school
Knowing when they get home
They can jump in the pool.

So many people
Are angry about life
Shortage of money
Causes worry and strife.

We must live, let live
Sincere thoughts of many
Sometimes thinking of others
Not worth a penny

Ten in our family
We thought life was great
There was always a
Birthday to celebrate

Now problems of war
When will it end
May each everywhere whisper
Amen.

LIFE

People are humanity
We meet on any day
Working, jogging
Happily going along their way.

A waving hand, hi or hello
Might help them realize
The same sun shines on everyone
Regardless of their size.

We all have relatives
Scattered 'round this wondrous land
A smile will speak volumes about
Knowledge, life is grand.

Perhaps a prayer
For the young and older
They were also babies
Cuddled on a shoulder.

Many have no one
To whom they might turn
Maybe today in a small way
You make it your concern.

WHY

Good morning, good night
Said each morning and night
All across our land
Because it is our culture
Not at anyone's demand.
When will some in our country
Know what to do how to live
We were taught in childhood
How to forget, forgive.

I realize terrorists
Struck our United States
Many people killed and hurt
No reason to start a war
If leaders had been alert
Many lives have been given
At a monumental cost
Many of our citizens
Feel all is lost.

The entire world has leaders
Trying to protect their land
From greed, power, spending billions
Is difficult to understand.
Many prayers are said
Pray God, don't leave us alone
War will end, peace will come
Bring our soldiers home.

MEMORIES OF MOM — 1930

When you bring joy to others
It will make your heart sing
When the cold of winter leaves
You realize soon it will be spring.

Daffodils and crocus through the ground
Tulips soon make their presence known
And roses with thorny needles
In their glory will be shown.

Cosmos, marigolds, petunias
Pansies in glorious display
Zinnias, iris and forget-me-nots
Snapdragons line the drive way.

Flowering trees soon follow
Cherry, peach, apple and pear
Then the specials, strawberries,
Blackberries, raspberries,
Picked along the railroad right of way.

We could go to the forests
For violets, thorny jump-ups too
Chain white daisies by the dozens
Yellow dandelions with green to stew.

Today this things means nothing
Their memories few if any
When we took too many to mom
Giving to neighbors, we would get a penny.

NATURE

I like the sunrise each morning
Dew like crystals on the lawn
Softly the wind is blowing
Hibiscus attract the doe and fawn.

They love the blossoms and leaves
Growing around our pool
The deer follow each other
Like children going to school.

It causes aggravation
To some neighbors along the street
Yet animals are a part of God's creation
And when hungry, they will eat.

Our backyard a work of art
Don works out there each day
When the animals come, we welcome them
They usually disappear in May.

They are found in many states
Across the land near and far
When you read a sign "Deer Crossing"
Take warning, hitting one will wreck your car.

THE FEW

Having wandered many miles
Life has been a pleasure
With wave of hand, glad hello
Leaving memories to treasure.

People learn the beauty
When enjoying each new day
May it bring them closer
To life in every way.

Let not your heart grow weary
Love will ne'er neglect the few
Weave a net of real devotion
Your angel will follow you.

For all the years traveled
You showed pride in life
Now enjoy the highways—byways
Every moment without strife.

FAITH

I wonder as I ponder
About the musings everyday
Who owns the air we breathe
Or earth we walk along our way.

The power we have in us
May cause pain or show delight
Something we might dwell on
Before our eyes close each might.

Was it good news you heard today
Or thoughts that gave you pride
Easing feelings of discontent
Could be faith was on your side.

Remember if trust you show
To one close or far away
Imagine dreams cost you nothing
Nor does the road you trod today.

DID YOU

Did you ever

Count each minute

Waste an hour

Say what's the use

Cause someone sorrow

Fail to understand

Feel the fool

Neglect to wave your hand

Did you just be cool.

Did you ever

Try to count the stars

Or see the man in the moon

Walk in puddles after a heavy rain

Makes images out of clouds on high

If so, why, oh why....

DAYS

Don plants trees and shrubs
Around our home on Foxfords Chase
The lawn is mowed to perfection
Jade green, everything in place.

Our pool blue as sapphire
Flowers bloom pink, red, white
Cars shine in brilliant color
All things done just right.

Sometimes we drive the Corvette
To a small town named DeLand
We do a little shopping there
Stetson's campus is really grand.

Wednesday, Thursday, Friday
We attend Mass at seven
Father Grasso the celebrant
Enjoy his talks briefly given.

Attending Lourdes, St Brendan, St. Paul
Sometimes Prince of Peace
Offering prayers where needed
Pray soon the wars will cease.

GRAND PRIZE

I believe in dreaming
Dreams do not cost a cent
If they did I would spend a dime
So they would keep me company
For a long, long time.

A wanderer out of nowhere
Might pass along your way
To a journey out of loneliness
His clothes in disarray.

May his spirit keep him happy
May life find a big surprise
So when he reaches a road to travel
He will have a happy day
Winning the grand prize.

DO YOU

Do you recall high button shoes
In zero winter weather
Buckle overshoes, hip boots
Made of genuine leather.

Do you recall
Chopping wood, carrying in coal
Gathering kindling to start a fire
Things remind, am I old.

Do you remember gathering eggs
Milking a cow in the barn
Heating bricks to warm you feet
Freezing toes could cause harm.

Do you remember
Skating on a frozen pond
Or mom baking bread doughnuts by the dozens
Which we were very fond.

Do you remember snow ice cream
Horse and buggy days
Or a team hitched to a sleigh
Adorned with bells ringing
We used bales of hay.

Do you remember
All these things
So may I be so bold
You join my years of ninety
My grandchildren say
Grandma, are you getting old.

IDEAS

I found hope in
Everyone shopping at
The grocery store
A card to bring happiness
As I walked in the door

I forgot energy
Skipped by temptation
Found ideas on a shelf
How to aid a foreign nation
I tried to conquer loneliness
Saw a shiny star
Which made me feel
Reality was in a tiny jar.

Hum a tune while browsing
Share a smile when you begin
A ray of imagination
Could never be a sin
Buy a candy bar to relish
Or chew gum for relaxation
A tummy needs nourishment
And decreases anxious vexation.

TALK

Sing a tune
As you walk
Stop a minute
For small talk

Turn around
Walk right back
Know your mind
Is not losing track

You just did
A friendly deed
For one who
Really was in need.

THOSE WERE THE DAYS

I used to visit when mom
Went to the grocery store
Read the labels on everything
To learn what they were for

Seeing sacks of sugar, flour
Pickles in a barrel, ten cents each
Things high up above
With a sliding ladder one could reach.

I saw potatoes, apples, melons
That a farmer brought everyday
Took their value out in groceries
No money changed hands that way.

Castor oil, olive oil, salve of every kind
Cough syrup of vanilla flavor
Rows of many candy jars
Licorice sticks were a life savor.

Eggs from chickens, ducks, geese
Some very large in praise
They sold these to hatcheries
For chicks later folks would raise.

I thought of patience man must have
Like the seed that he had sown
If his harvest was successful
Might add a room to his home.

[THOSE WERE THE DAYS—continued]

Everything was kept in order
Scrubbed floors, windows clean
Oilcloth by the yard was sold
To keep your table clean.

I learned many years ago
Trust was a serious thing
If anything ever happened
You gave the old wall phone a long ring.

Those were the horse and buggy days
We also had a "Model T"
We would pile in on Saturday night
To go to a ten cent movie.

We were a large family
And a very happy bunch
If anyone was there at noon
They were asked to stay for lunch.

Kids, young folks have many things today
Add to more than one can measure
A trip way back in time
Would be something each might treasure.

FRIENDHIP

I awakened in the midst of night
To a strange and eerie feeling
There was silence everywhere
My memory began reeling.

Thinking of the happiness
From a full year of delight
I said a prayer of thanksgiving
As daylight took o'er the night.

My thought could I give back
The pleasures I have known
About many years of friendship
To people whom I've known.

I wish that love be scattered
Reach everyone this day
Blessings of peace and joy
Follow who strayed today.

Guardian angels follow each
Tenderly watch o'er all
Guiding us by day and night
Help when we stumble and fall.

WEAVE

All who walk the path of life
Not stumble on the way
If so ask God to help
Listen he will say
Look around you will see
The key to happiness
Is following you today
Pause a moment
There is beauty everywhere
The air you breathe, health receive
Angels guard with care
So weave a life of doing, caring
Each day be sure to give
A thought making something great
For someone else to live.

SPIRIT

Do you ever think a spirit
Is following you around
Fills you with contentment
Believe your steps don't touch the ground.

Sincerity is strong belief
A treasure to behold
An angel brought the message
Saying I return to the fold.

I neglected many times
In years now long past
To ask forgiveness now is the time
As life hastens very fast.

Trust I kneel on bended knee
All my sins to tell
Wondering if the Master
Knows all is not well.

WIFE — CHILD

You have gone and left me
I get lonely everyday
Darling I keep hoping
You'll come back to me someday.

We wanted home and family
When you went away to serve
For our grand old country
And you never lost your nerve.

Come back tomorrow my darling
Always my wish will be
You will get tired of wandering
And come back tomorrow to me.

I hope you soon remember
We had such a wonderful life
I keep wishing darling
You'll come home to your baby and wife.

FRIDAY

It's Friday and my day
To take a little stroll
I hope no one will bother me
I won't tell a soul.
Just put on my walking boots
Be happy and care free.

Leave my worries safe at home
Hidden on a shelf
Meet someone new, walk with them
Or mope along all by myself.

I might even write a song
Or jot down a line of poetry
Maybe climb a hill
Gaze at beauty surrounding me.

Listening to a whippoorwill
Soon its time to return home
Tomorrow walk to the sea
Take a stroll, watch the waves roll
In these boots you had made for me.

MY HANDS

I look at my hands, true servants they are
More agile than any machine by far.
These hands do things no other can
For each days work, I must plan.
These hands, obedient, ready to serve
Doing more for me than I deserve.
They never question how the job is run
They stay and toil until work is done.
Sometimes the chore is easy, leaving strength to spare
Then times of hard work, difficult to bear
All the hard knocks impact on their frame
They willingly stay by me just the same.
I owe a lot to these hands of mine
I'm glad for them, they suit me fine
Never without them everyday
Thank God my hands help me on life's way.

REMEMBERING CARNEGIE

I went to a school, not sent there by force
To enjoy life fully from well chartered course
Walking, standing or sitting, these lessons will guide
Follow the pink book and do so with pride.

One instructor Miss Florence I recall
Very gracious with kindness for all
Frances Pound with her brogue, must have come from the south
She speaks her eyes twinkle, a smile frames her mouth.

Mary Sedekum gets attention when she takes the stand
Dorothea Doetsch with a gleaming diamond on her left hand
All these instructors are very sincere
They drive quite a distance to teach us here.

We have nurses, housewives, secretaries too
A piano teacher, bookkeeper, toy counselor ooooh
Could we get a discount Irene, if we tried
Money from Wilma Steidley's bank on the side.

We may see Alice Meier for a dinner by jove
Or see Mary Alice for a fancy new stove
Say Vickie, could you teach me the do-re-mi-
We asked Lois Watson, is federal housing free.

To Ruth Sprinkel for gravel or a truck full of sand
May Aleshire could nurse us, there's a person real grand.
Buelah Crouch a housewife, what could be better
Unless we drove to Taylorville visit Shirley Etter.

JoAnn Calandrino a secretary who works for our state
Fran Harms a keen housewife makes employers wait

If our car needs some oil, to Barb Huddleston we'll go
Then drive to South College, visit Paula Pidcoe.

Wilma Davison another housewife, tiny and sprite
Norma Blue a nurse, call her day or night
The entire class roster I've enjoyed every one
Especially the visit to Ruth's new little home.

It can't be just six years, won't you all agree
That spit curls were popular, I would be just twenty three
Come on Mrs. Ryder, if this is the truth
You must have been drinking from the fountain of youth.

I feel the progress I made will last all my life
Being interested in learning, heeding good sound advice
I'll try to grow as through life I go
Share the knowledge I gained, keep my memories aglow.

Here's to all my acquaintances, I met at this school
The best life has to offer, a valuable rule
Those lessons so helpful, they taught us to smile
With sincerity, honesty, genuine style
These are great weeks of action packed fun you'll see
Let Dorothy Carnegie help be happy and carefree.

ADS

Advertising
By mail, computer, TV
Do they think
Money comes from
A tree?

JACKY JOE

August eleven twenty-o-five
A new friend came to visit
A tiny five pound Schnauzer
Into everything he sees
Makes me wonder what it is
We have name him Jacky Joe
Which could be JJ for short
When he grabs his teddy bear
You should hear him snort
Four white paws, coat of shiny black
Cropped ears, tail, beautiful eyes
He will make life worthwhile
Like the sun, moon and starry skies
I did not say from the start
He is only ten weeks old
After only four days with us
Soon all lives will unfold
He eats well, runs throughout the house
Answers to his name on call
Soon he will be a challenge
And great pleasure to one and all.

REMINISCING

Yesterday I sat thinking
About nineteen thirty-two
The year my eighteenth birthday
Since then I added quite a few.

Seems years go rapidly
Tho days and months are long
Just try keeping hands busy
Saying prayers, singing a song

Each of us get lonesome
About the years we have seen
There is a god who understands
As we follow him in a dream.

Let our yesterdays and tomorrows
Pave the path for young and old
Fill your days with expectations
Keeping memories on hold.

OUR HOMELAND

A New Year twenty-o-five
Has arrived in splendorous glory
Two thousand four a disastrous
Time for thousands
Many lived to tell the story.

We must realize God never
Gives more than we can stand
Although many the questions
What is happening in our land.

There are those who cause problems
Affecting homes in all places
An issue than concerns me
Children's small sad faces.

USA known for freedom
Some do their very best
Our troops are dying every day
Their request.

So people who believe in God
All across this wonderful nation
Say a prayer everyday
Bring them home for a grand celebration.

ASHLAND, ILLINOIS

I remember Ashland, Illinois
Of many years ago
They call is a village
To me a small town on the go.

Doctor, dentist, banks, trucking
Dry good store, Hexters the name
Drug store run by Brownbacks
Danenbergers the grocers, not a chain.

Movie house, firehouse, jewelers
Churches, tonsorial parlors, grain elevators
With bins to store the farmer's crops
Then reload it on the freighters.

Antique shop, gas stations, café
Cobbler, schools for education
Sixty or seventy years ago
Folks did not travel far
To enjoy a vacation.

Must not forget the restaurant
Where one could enjoy a coke
Or the Ashland sentinel
Sometimes would share a joke.

Saturday night folks came to town
You could meet all your neighbors
All would come to visit
Farmers getting away from their labors.

Memories of Ashland
With a hi or hello
Where we could spend our ten cents
Make olden days overflow.

WISHING

Have you often wished
You could board a ship
Sail the seven seas
Spend money like it grew on trees
Purchasing everything you please.

Visiting countries far and wide
Islands what a delight
England, Scotland, Ireland
Watching bag pipers quite a sight

Scenery of famous Switzerland
Austria with the finest glass
Must not forget Wales and Italy
How quickly our time passed.

Germany with their steins of beer
Extremely heavy to hold
At the Hofbrau we visited
We stayed the night to unfold.

Hungary and Budapest
With untold treasures we could buy
Put these places on your list
Before life passes you by.

TEN FOXFORDS CHASE

We live in sunny Florida
Known throughout the land
Sure we have some hurricanes
And tides that wash away our sand.

Our home on route forty
Three miles west of I-95
Living here is wonderful
Keeping home and lawn with pride.

Jacksonville on the north
Orlando, Disney, south and west
Places to go, things to see
If education is your quest.

When you come to visit
Like our friends form England, Australia or Germany
We entertain American style
Food from each country.

So take a chance, come visit
There are interesting things to see
We treat all like family
In Ormond Beach near the sea.

FLORIDA 2003

Dick & Betty came to visit
In January twenty-o-three
February came, we had great times
'en though she had a painful knee.

Therapy three times a week
Which was a vacation well planned
To enjoy Florida sunshine
And get a rest, also a tan!

Don's friend, therapist, Manuel
He is really quite a guy
If ever I need his service
I'll give him a try.

Then came the rain, some not needed
It happened not by request
Oh, well just wear a happy smile
Keeping dry, umbrellas did their best.

Alfie's in Ormond by the Sea
It was just so-so
Red Lobster did their usual fare
One of the best I know.

Sweetwater's was a gourmet treat
A real great place to eat
Ocala saw us at Carmichaels
But the LPGA Country Club can't be beat.

Hungarian Village may be over rated
But noon at Frappes was lunch divine
We've saved some real good places
When they return another time.

For culture at Daytona Playhouse
We saw "Kiss Me Kate"
Put on by local talent
They're not fabulous, but great!

Norwood's did a gracious job
With service that's just grand
Food and drinks enjoyed
The waiter well in command.

Billy's served a lovely meal
Don and Frances did not go
The energy they both possess
Seldom ever they say no.

Breakfasts at Bob Evans
For Dick and Betty what a treat
No eggs or bacon on those days
But sausage and fried mush to eat.

The Ale House in Sanford
We traveled one sunny day
Better places we had chosen
It was just okay.

Peach Valley where they dined alone
Sometime I'll give it a try.
One of the greatest treats of all
Was Publix coconut custard pie.

We drove to Flagler Beach pier
For breakfast one fine day
The rain came pouring down
There we did not stay.

Drove a while longer in precipitation
What a messy situation
Finally wind up to feast
At the Halifax Plantation.

One of the best places where we ate
Always served with style and grace
We sat down to a sumptuous meal
At Ten Foxfords Chase.

Dick worked at Daytona Speedway
Feeding hot dogs to the best
Standing on your feet all day
Can put you to the test.

Then bikers arrived by the thousands
Traveling many a mile
Some even from foreign lands
On bikes of every style.

[FLORIDA 2003—continued]

They saw Spring Breakers come to town
To celebrate and worship sun in style
It does seem just a bit ridiculous
Hardly wear more than a smile.

And of course we went to Mass
St. Brendan's, Lourdes and St. Paul
At Korona, Ormond and Daytona Beach
Dear friend, Fr. Grasso, the best of all.

All too soon time to call it a day
And weave their way back home
We will find new places to dine
Next time they decide to roam.

A safe trip back to Palatine
In only two days time
Guess David's corned beef and cabbage
Is what got them there just fine.

LOVELY TIMES

Lovely times lovely places
May be found in happy faces
Small things being loyal make
Happiness each day you wake.

Reach to all you meet
Your heart feels an extra beat
Never will you walk alone
Laughter may always fill your home.

Greet a neighbor go to lunch
Grasp a hand in gentle touch
Chase loneliness every day
Smiles keep heartache away.

Say goodbye to angry feelings
Show them you are a friend
Find that all tomorrows
Bring joy that never ends.

Today I will reach out and touch
Someone that cares so much
All will enjoy a better day
A guardian angel leads the way.

EACH YEAR

January—starts each new year
February—tells us St. Valentine's day to near
March—St. Pat's day is on the wing
April—tulips and daffodils sprouting spring
May—Mother's Day best friend you ever had
June—celebrate Father's Day with your dad
July—fireworks show up at night
August—sometimes the hottest days a fright
September—finds all back in school
October—Halloween costumes kids think they're cool
November—celebrate Thanksgiving with a turkey so grand
December—remember what Christmas really means
The birth of our savior Jesus, king of kings.

LIFE — 2006

Many miles I have traveled
Glorious sights I've seen
When a good friend dies
The pain it leaves
Causes memories of a life once serene.
Where you travel what you've seen
Leaves an empty feeling
Get off your duff
So life is tough
Feeling sadness is not appealing
Many folks have sadness
How about our service men
Peace is what they're after
Sit down write a few lines
Back when you were in school
Be a friend lend a hand
May you recall the golden rule
In my nineties I often wonder
Many times what's the use
Then I think of the less fortunate
The war causes so much abuse
So people pray every day
Our country is in devastation
With a feeling of love in your heart
Seek new people to rule our nation.

THINK ABOUT IT

There are hurricanes, tornadoes, fires, floods
Putting people in great distress
Accidents on the highways taking lives
Many searching for happiness.
Send a message to a loved one
Whether close or far away
Let them know you're thinking of them
Hoping good things make their day.
We all need to be remembered
By someone, somewhere, sometime
Reach out a friendly hand shake
Might ease a troubled mind.

REMEMBER

Given life in a country
Known as land of the free
A great chance to love and live
Learn right from wrong, forget forgive.

Instilled with hope and happiness
By an angel to each you see
Blessings sent be faithful
Assisting mortals such as me.

Given voice in what we say
Accept all things that come our way
Fill the land with families rare
Scatter them around everywhere.

Greet each with a happy smile
Showing kindness it's worthwhile
Remembering if they should stray
Love gives strength, makes them stay.

Someone is watching over you
Knows kind deeds that you do
At days ending say a prayer
Remember God is everywhere.

FLORIDA OUR NEW HOME

Built a home in Hunter's Ridge
Moved to Ormond Beach
Number 10 Foxfords Chase
No area could be more magic
Good neighbors with style and grace
We have Ursula and J.J.
Bob and Fran close by
Margot across the street
Joan at Six with her three Labs
Rascal, Scamp and Mischief.
Then Bill and Jennifer
A great couple to meet
Then Don and I at our perfect Ten
With Ed and Judy next door.
Bill and Bennie at Fourteen
She is my state quarter queen.
Around the corner are Frank and Barbara
Including Jacky's friend Sundance
Across the street now Jack and Glenda
Then Casey, Sandy and Mike and Georgia
Next our newest neighbor Marilyn Rice
And her handsome Schnauzer Sparky
One door west the Clymers from Iowa
Ned, Danielle, Clint and Colby
Then Al and Janice, Anisha and Michael
Moved here from Michigan.
We love Hunter's Ridge
With deer, dogs and cats and kids
Nice lakes and beautiful birds
Like living in a park

The good Lord blessed us all
In daylight and dark.

2006

Gentle rain is falling
Sun lights the eastern sky
Soon the day will brighten
Giving earth a chance to dry.
New life given to everything
Awakened trees are listening
Gift of showers from above
Each blade of grass glistening
Children very happy
No school for a week
Thanksgiving day is coming
Turkey a real treat
Soon another day dawns
Filled with Christmas cheer
Gifts, trimmed trees, ornaments
Family you hold dear
Then a new year beckons
Memories over flow
Twenty 06 passed quickly
My prayer
'Peace On Earth" will grow.

AN ODE TO CHARLIE

We meet people everyday
As through life we trod
One of the great for Don and me
His name Charlie Cobb.
Living at number six on Foxfords Chase
With Joan, Scamp, Rascal, Missy
When going for a walk
You'd have to keep their pace.
His game of golf important
He would arise each morn
Travel many miles some days
To reach his destination
Arriving with much determination.

Charlie was more than a neighbor
He was a friend tried and true
Working in many a foreign place
I feel he greeted everyone graciously
Regardless of their race.
Charlie did not ever complain
Of the burden he had to bare
Having a great outlook on life
He suffered more than his share.
I know God answers prayers
In heaven where Charlie now dwells

My lighted candle flickers
As his angel rings the bells.
Charlie, we still love you
Knowing you will wait
Patiently with a big hello
When we reach the golden gate.
The sun now shines for you each day
You make eagles, birdies or par
Doing what you loved on earth
We'll be watching from afar.

IMOGENE AND HENRY

As you travel on your journey
Have some fun along the way
As the Camry clicks off the miles and pace
Remember, home is still the greatest place.

Don and I wish the very best
When visiting family
A prayer is said, a candle lit
To keep you company.

So have a good time while away
Travel safely, this we pray
We will welcome your return
That will be a happy day.

May the good Lord bless and keep you,

Frances

THE ORLANDOS TRAVELING

Z   zoom along the highway

Y   you will wear a smile

X   extra time in recalling

W   what makes life worthwhile

V   very often we ponder

U   using our memories

T   today will soon be tomorrow

S   seeking a chance to please

R   resting a while from travel

Q   question how far will we go

P   plans were made for this journey

O   only miles seem long and slow

N   never a mistake in packing

M   making everything fit snug and tight

L   luck was in the arranging

K   knowing things would work out right

J   joy is forever in giving

I   *Imogene* and *Henry* side by side

H   happy to visit family and friends

G   God goes along for the ride

F   friends they are forever

E   each day Don and I realize

D   doing for others a treasure

C   caring in worth the grand prize

B   blessing the friendship we enjoy

A   as early for weekday Mass we arise.

08/20/02

TO BETTY WITH LOVE

You've celebrated your eightieth
I heard you were aghast
You enjoyed all the festivities
Now wonderful memories to last.

Diane planned a beautiful party
For her mother's celebration
The mirror shows you're not that age
Blame it on imagination.

Things come in jars and bottles
For the toe nails and finger tips
Add a little glow for cheeks
A touch of red for smiling lips.

If someone says you are getting old
Never feel despair
With knowledge that's outstanding
You may even do your hair.

Dick a champion companion
You have been a wonderful wife
Many do not have these blessings
That last throughout their life.

You have a darling daughter
Who knows how great you are
Sons, grandchildren, nieces and nephews
Leave impressions like shining stars.

Such memories are gifts of love
From people who attended
Don and I would have been there

The eye surgeon said no travel
Our idea soon shattered, ended.

Stay as you are Betty dear
Being honored a delight
Store up memories to treasure
Show all, eighty is a worthwhile fight.

Come visit anytime you wish
Put all worries on the shelf
Be kind, be loving, good health enjoy
Most of all just be yourself.

God Bless You Betty,

Frances

EMOTION

Start on a journey
From Florida to cities
Like Atlanta. Georgia
Building there sure pretty
Next stop Nashville, Tennessee
Opryland found there
Happiness, fun and pleasure
People from many countries
Visiting everywhere.
Singing songs many first rate
Educational, mountains, knowledge
Ride the choo-choo it's great
Be off to Kentucky-Louisville
Enjoy blue grass, horses, famous derby
Known everywhere
Thousands entertained with care
Finally we reach Illinois
Springfield then Chicago
Baseball Cubs known for games
When playing St. Louis Cardinals
Also known for fame
I still have many living
All across the land
From Belleville to Arlington Heights
Winter's ice and snow I couldn't stand.

EYES

Where did I go
What did I do
When did I smile
Bid someone adieu
With eyes to see
Hands to touch
Foolish questions
Never ask how much
Greet people kindly
Enjoy a hello
Easing pain
Helps faces glow
Good, kind gentleness
Keeps one's mind alert
Speak words with anger
Feelings are hurt
Greetings share
Make tomorrow brighter
Yesterday's passed
Burdens lighter.

PATH

The path of life beckons
Someone who will stray
Across fields and meadows
Thoughts miles away

Wild flowers blooming everywhere
Trees showing leaves
Birds building nests
Wherever they please.

Small animals enjoy a small brook
Squirrels, rabbits enjoyed with delight
School out for summer abounds
All games to enjoy
Love playing baseball
Or fishing from ponds.

A poet has the urge writing
Books that have promise, praise
Remembering things of years passed
As one reads each page.

I will keep on wandering
Back to recanting years
History, travel, family, friends
Thoughts of parents, teachers, peers.

EVERY YEAR

January—First month each year
All folks enjoy saying "Happy New Year"

February—Valentine's celebration
Cards send around the nation

March—Warmer weather is grand
A good time visiting Ireland

April—We expect many showers
For growing tulips, daffodils, all spring flowers

May—Mothers enjoy celebrations
Gifts, cards, candy received with appreciation

June—Dad's day buy him a gift
A new golf bag will give him a lift

July—Fireworks, lots of noise
Time dad acts like one of the boys

August—a month to rejoice
Jumping in the pool a very good choice

September—maybe not so good as a rule
For children returning to school

October—Halloween with appear
Trick or treating happens each year

November—turkey time the king
Pumpkin pie, mince, cranberries give a zing

December—Santa's coming to bring delight
Everyone waiting, on eve of glorious night.

TRUTH

Wishing to conquer,
Holding a session
Speaking quietly
A wonderful lesson.

THE VINE

A highway might bring happiness
Paved with good intention
Occupy your mind
Treasure find
Great enough to mention

Sailing on a steamship
Seas of sapphire blue
Leisurely contentment
Bound to follow you.

Others find fascination
Lasting a longtime
I like the enchantment
Drinking a glass
Of juice made from the vine.

TREASURED ELF

A little time erases
Problems from your mind
When neighbors need assistance
Remember to be kind
Sunny skies will brighten
Moon glows, stars shimmer
Birds building nests in trees
Nestlings hatching need their dinner.

Spring's in the air soon
Folks are aware
Reunions, picnics, celebrations
Plans for Disneyworld etcetera
Some to foreign nations.

Each day taken pleasantly
Bring smiles no sad faces
Washing unhappiness away
Created by God's graces.

Never feel what's the use
Feel no sorrow for yourself
The tiny voice heard whispering
Could be a treasured elf.

SIX MONTHS

Having walked a lonely path
On a cold wintry day
Wishing soon spring arrives
Ides of March not far away.

Hibiscus flowering brilliant red
Trees showing tiny leaves
Cardinals, mocking birds, whippoorwills
Butter flies, honey bees.

Folks around speaking of peace
Authorities saying in months
War would soon be over
Like looking for a miracle
Finding a four leaf clover.

Why is there so many flaws
Given in their speeches
Expecting humanity to believe
Stupidity, reaches.

Look at numbers lost everywhere
Lives so quickly given
Fathers, mothers, sisters, brothers
And the dollars more than several billion.

WANDERING

I start wandering again
Around the U.S.A.
Starting in California, Nevada
The slot machine payday.
Arizona next in line,
Visit Utah state
Majestic grounds of Mormon temple
Worth time you wait.
Off to Idaho harvest potatoes
Oregon next in line
Will you find tomatoes
You might pick from a vine.
Nebraska a place west they say
So is Oklahoma, New Mexico, Texas
Largest in all United States
Let's hope they all pay taxes
North and South Dakota, North and South Carolina
Ohio, Iowa, Illinois, Kansas, Indiana, Alabama
During cold weather they wear a bandana.
New York, New Jersey, New Hampshire, Maine
Louisiana, Massachusetts, Pennsylvania
Touch liberty with your hand
Washington, Wisconsin, Connecticut, Delaware, Kansas
Rhode Island, Vermont, Mississippi, Tennessee
Kentucky, Georgia, you'll find a pecan tree
Missouri, Montana, Minnesota, Colorado
West Virginia, Virginia, Florida, Hawaii, Alaska
Doing the hula, come back—Visit you all
Everyone will ask.

ENTERTAINMENT

Countless sports folks enjoy
At times need invitations
People by thousands travel
Across USA and foreign nations.

Race cars, motorcycles, baseball, tennis
Basketball, soccer, golf, ice hockey
Dancing, skiing, swimming, skating, boxing
Sailing, surfing, canoeing, snow boarding
Many of these good exercise
None of which I'm pursuing
Poker games, playing cards, gambling
On the high seas lose my money
I do not invest very much moola
Never did like losing
Used to scoring 200 many times bowling
Fly a plane, drive mph 95
Received a ticket one time only going 45
Law stated much safer
75 the amount, I read in the paper
more places to go, things to see, a poet on the go
as age creeps, someone said
see, I told you so.

DUTIES

Who is the someone following
When many times I stray
Sometimes a flawless memory
Leaves a minute to pray
Days pass rapidly
Visiting neighbors at the fence
You wave bye-bye as cars pass by
Phone rings, rush in caller with nonsense
Finish working in the house
Return, pull weeds
Feed chickens, ducks, geese, turkeys
Told your doing good deeds.
Returning inside there's laundry
Scrub floors, wash windows, dusting
Doing this every day, disgusting.
Baking break, cookies, frying donuts
Then all favorites in family
Now everything's bought
At the super mart
'nuff said, not like it used to be
Keeping one's hands happy
Much of life depends
Take care of yourself
Love of doing never ends.

SEA AND SEE

Having a lighthouse in our state
Down Ponce inlet way
More beautiful than many
Found in the USA.
Gift shop brochures
Filled with information
About shipwrecks years ago
In this part of our nation.
Climb steps to the top
The Atlantic viewed far and wide
Finding a place to rest
When reaching top with pride.
Visit down our way anytime
On vacation, see sandy beaches ocean blue
Shrimp boats searching for nets filled
Then find other things to do.
A boat down the river, alligators, eagle nests
Manatees, the captain's entertainment
Relax, enjoy the rest on returning
Stop in Deland, Stetson University
Enjoy campus building grand
Return to Daytona, don't forget Embry Riddle
The Speedway or Mainland High
Historic Basilica of St. Paul on Ridgewood Avenue
Stop inside, a beautiful sight to view.
On to St. Augustine, oldest city
Take a few minutes rest
Enjoy your stay
Florida at its best.

RUSS

My brother Russell Sherwood
Fourth son of mom and dad
Happy as an infant
Growing up a mighty lad.

Always liked doing things
His hobby making sling shots
Could hit a sparrow
With a small stone ker-plop!

Grown to manhood he came
To live with Joe and me
Found a job to keep busy
An old car to drive around
Calling it his tin Lizzie.

Soon found a girl friend Dorothy
Had to work a little harder
Because deciding to get married
Needed more to fill the larder.

He and Dorothy issued two girls, two boys
Filled their hearts with pleasure
Kathleen, Barbara, Greg and Donald
Many happy times to treasure.

Kathleen and Barb attended
Sacred Heart Academy
Greg and Don attended Feitshans
Loved baseball to the nth degree.

Too soon Russell was called to heaven
In 1972 when only fifty-six.

The Master took him home
Dorothy died some years ago
Her angel came to get her
Now in heaven with Russell
They are not alone.

2006

Days are getting short
Winter time is near
Florida other sates
No hurricanes this year
Evenings bring darkness
Giving time to relax
Habits become problems
Gaining weight, eating snacks
Some days to Mass I go
Arriving around seven
Listening to Father Grasso
His intellectual messages briefing given
May all attending worthy be
Go about their day
My prayer being answered
Help someone who might stray.

BUDS

Buds blossoming to flowers
On sunny warm spring days
Soon butterflies, bees
Gathering nectar
Cause the hummingbird
To fly away.

CHOICE

Still around writing poetry
Life I enjoy
Seeing friends pursuing
Delight in their voice
Sharing knowledge, learning
Gratifying marvelous choice
Looking at life
Thrilling to see
Smiles on their faces
Eyes glowing in mystery
Travel the world
For education, success
Seeing children happy
Parents we bless
Neighbors passing by
Wave of their hand
Happy we are living
Proudly we stand
Travel by plane train
Ship, bus or car
A beacon searching
The brightest star
If life gets bumpy
Along the road
There is someone to
Help you carry the load.

GOODBYE

My dreams
Mine along
Matter not
Where I roam
Traveling onward
Kind to all I meet
Why not stop, visit
Rest body, mind and feet.
Reaching hands
In friendship
Give each a smile
Treat them with
A joyous greeting
They will find
A smile in style
Winter passes
Say goodbye
Comes spring
Getting anxious
See earth filled
With growing things
Doing what I like best
Hope seeds planted
Are soon grown
Then the flowers
Will burst into bloom.

LEARNING

Learning to love
Learning to care
Knowledge of learning
Never unfair
Learning to give
Learn to excel
Expertise in learning
In life you dwell
Learning to read
Believe in yourself
Color of humanity
May each enjoy good health
Did God ever say
What color we be
Living, loving learning
Important to me
Learn to spell
Words come our right
When you have learned
Makes life a delight
School is for learning
Spelling, math, proper reading
Soon you're realizing
Being educationally succeeding.

LIFE

Many times think
About what you do
Return full measure
Treasure life through
Job being difficult
Put energy in it
Precious time wasted
Worth more than a minute
Look for one lonely
Share a smile
Find they qualify
Making days worthwhile.

EARTH

Trees showing leaves
Birds butterflies bees
Getting nectar from flowers
Scatter immediately
From April showers
The almighty created
A marvelous earth
Hoping all enjoy
Land of their birth.

NADA

If you like shopping
Viewing something precious
Make no suggestion
Unless intent on buying
A foolish question.

THANK YOU

Ne'er let a day pass
Saying thank you God
Knowledge, accomplishment
Wasted if beneath the sod.

SO WHAT

Back aches, shoulder pain
Legs are swollen too
Use a walker getting around
Not a fun thing to do
Also have hearing aids
Missing words inane
Eye sight great since surgery
View everything again
If you feel wine, champagne
Seem to be shocking
Not me at ninety three
Better than nylon stockings.

DAYS END

Pondering, wondering
Abut yesterday
Saying "Hi you all"
Make your day
Will you be truthful
At days end
Someone asks a favor
May on you depend.

NO

Do not hurt feelings
Flirt with temptations
Say something wrong
Angers relations.

WRONG

Do things wrong
Make their right
Your day brightens
With sheer delight.

TIM

Tim said to me
Put on your left shoe first
I did, then laughing he said
What are you going to do
With the one that's left.

BUSH

Ring around the rose bush
Wanting to pick a posy
Be careful how you do it
You could get a thorn in your nosey.

NO HURRRY

Fifty years ago
Life moved slow
Seemed no reason to hurry.
Now things are done
E-mail, computer, phone, fax
Look at time saved
Figuring your income tax.

PLAN

Plan to help
Someone achieve
Knowledge gained
Maybe theirs to succeed.

BEE

The butter fly and the bumble bee
Were flying from the flowers
Suddenly a tiny bird
Lit on a blossom higher
Saying I will not bother you
Nectar up here plentiful
And I reach flowers too
Look, admire
Soon they began to search about
Finding more to please
Bumble bee starting
Pestering humming bird to tease
Deciding cautiously
Saying have your fun
This game I won, hee-hee
I'm dining with a monarch
Even though just a bee.

HERE'S TO THE HEROES (1998)

Here's to the heroes so gallantly brave
Volusia and Flagler they united to save
Firemen, police, volunteers, doctors and nurses
Houligan's and Daytona 500 opened their purses.

Clergy, churches, businesses, the National Guard too
Donations poured in from me and from you
Newspapers, TV, radio gave up their time
Telephone workers kept us on-line.

Tired and weary with mercy and might
Not one firefighter gave up the perilous fight.
From states represented all will acclaim
"The worse ever seen" was this inferno of flame.

Now drive along highways, forests are bare
We've so many to thank—and God did His share
There will be memories, laughter and mirth
And tales of fires that ravished our earth.

MARKUS

Steve and Marilyn
Came visiting
February 7, 2007
A wonderful couple
Who know how to live.
When we resided in Illinois
They were only two doors away
Now in Florida we enjoy their annual visits
We talk of lingering memories
To forever hold dear
About neighbors
Still living on Crestview drive
Because we moved to Ormond Beach
On 12-12-95.

Steve and Marilyn
Please keep in touch
By phone, letter
But personal visits are much better
Next time you're traveling our way
Hope you spend more than a day.

BALLOON

When all too soon
You want to swoon
Save your breath
Blow up a balloon

E OR I

Spelling Frances
No surprise
E is for girls
I for guys.

ANGER

Let not anger
Cause a frown
Keeps brows
Up not down.

SPRAY

Ring around the rosy
Jump rope game to play
Keep your arms close
You didn't use deodorant spray.

FEET

Learn to jump rope
May I repeat
Not land on your hind side
Always on your feet.

WINE

Feel the sensation
Being full of energy
You will find
The word energetic
In doing what you please
Walk a path of
Enchantment
A moment, minute or hour
Get your mind in gear
Don't scald yourself
Taking a shower
Never push the panic button
When you feel depressed
Settle your mind
With a glass of wine.

GARDENING

From the arbor filled with grapes
We used to pick
Mom would make jelly
Jam, seeding them not quick
Like hoeing rows of potatoes
Or getting worms from tomatoes
Starting rows of corn with kernels
Trying to mash up lumps of sod
Picking beans when ready
Carrots, beets,
Stop to get a lemon drink
Go back to the garden
Wish that it would rain
We might stop and think
Will the radishes be large enough
To pull again
A bunch, we might have for lunch
So plant a little garden
Give it lots of care
A good crop of veggies
With someone hungry you can share.

THINK

Did you ever stop
Think about reality
Like the rising of the sun
Moving across the universe
Setting when day is done
Why is the moon
Full in different stages
Shining overall the world
Lasting a million ages
Why the earth
Has seasons
Spring, summer, fall winter
Change of clothing weather
Needed to satisfy each wearer
Asking ourselves these questions
Why do people travel
Seeking sights of majesty
Helping minds and bodies unravel
I guess to put my mind at ease
Realizing generations
Thank god for all nations.

GREAT AND GREAT-GREAT GRANDCHILDREN

Stephanie the oldest
Graduated from Stetson in Deland
Works for an attorney
Willing to answer his demand.

Chelsea works part time
In Tallahassee
Attending Florida State University there
Hopes to become a pharmacist
A special student beyond compare.

Joey Clarke his name
Finished high school in May
Will enter college in the fall
Works and enjoys life each day.

Callahan Hood parents Karen & Spud
Sister Chelsea would like
Seeing his wish come true
Become a major league baseball player
As grandma I pray for this too

Now there's Chase and Maddison
Chase a student in pre-school
A good scholar age five
Maddison just six months old
Not issuing any rule.

JOYS

I shall write about
Grandchildren five
Each an inspiration
Taking life in stride
Karen the eldest
University schooled with pride

Rick has a business
Of his own
Taking care of lawns and shrubs
Don't ask what he does,
No work about grubs.

Tm a manager
At Gooding's grocery store
He has won many prizes
For creative displays
To beautify the store.

Denney another owner
HVAC installation and service
His chosen career
Has provided him purpose.

Tricia lives in Texas
An exec with Wachovia
Banking keeps her busy
Overseeing smany operations in stride
Via car, plane and taxis
Doing her duty staying occupied.

MY KITE

Did you ever try solving a mystery
Thoughtful wishing going down in history
Take a chance in summer 's July
Run with a kite with all your might
Seeing it fly majestically
Losing strips of cloth used for a tail
A bird grabbed it fast"
Just when starting to sail
Unhappiness, bewildered
When a sudden lurch, twine gave way
Disappointment, people laughed
Not funny because
Taking two hours making
No sympathy nor applause.

CONSTANTINOPLE

When in 5th grade at school
Long words were great
Learning to spell them
I liked to elongate,
A bad rainy morning
Teacher said take
Your tablet and write
A real long word.

Many wrote blackboard,
Ruler, pupil, heard, rainbow
One half hour later rain stopped
Bring your papers up
Bring in tomorrow's wood
Being the last to give her mine
I had carefully written
CONSTANTINOPLE.

She gazed at my paper, said
Where did you get this word
In a history book I replied
She said, "That's absurd
Can you spell it", my answer
I can sing it too
C o n s t a n t i n o p l e
Easy to spell as saying ABCs
Giving a sigh she gave a try
Con-stan-tin-ople she agreed
Soon the other students
Were singing along with me.

SERVICE

Live the life of a nomad
Traveling down the road
Notice the backpack he carries
Looking for someone who
Will give him a ride
Easing his heart ache
We picked up many in uniform
Traveling with heavy gear
During world war II
We stopped bought food for all
Take time to rest but do not
Be late for curfew.
Now you see them travel
With a small bag of clothes
If you do not have room
In the car
Give a couple of dollars
They will thank you
Help them travel far.

WORDS

Teaching others to spell at times was sheer delight
Many times a word's meaning can change out right:

Some—Sum	All—Awl
Wood—Would	An—Anne
Wine—Whine	Ate—Eight
Ware—Wear	Weight—Wait
Fair—Fare	Cane—Cain
Hear—Here	Be—Bee
Feet—Fete—Feat	Bail—Bale
No—Know	Beat—Beet
Maid—Made	Cheap—Cheep
Sale—Sail	Need—Knead
Shoe—Shoo	Main—Mane
Might—Mite	To—Too—Two
Flee—Flea	See—Sea
Weather—Whether	Loan—Lone
Write—Right	Which—Witch
Pray—Prey	Do—Dew
Mail—Male	Done—Dun
Gate—Gait	Flew—Flu
Son-Sun	Hi—High
Hair—hare	Great—Grate
Pear—Pare	Real—Reel
Knot—Not	Plain—Plane
Pain—Pane	Rain—Reign

Everyone can think of more but as we ponder
We may wonder

How do children understand
How can they learn
When not explained cautiously
Without making mistakes
Teachers must realize
Care it takes.

NUMB

Yesterday is over
Tomorrow never comes
Feelings about days, minutes, hours
Might make you feel numb
365 days, 12 months, 52 weeks
Seems bothersome
If feeling the minutes take up your time
Quality time leaves you numb.
Mention to friends, may I borrow
Seconds from you lasting one hour
Needing help ask one you know
Listen to plan—doing
When they finish talking
Problems not worth pursuing.

FACTS

Advertising disgusting
Especially for me
Places of business
Must think
We pick money from a tree.

AMEN

A nation's prayer
Sitting alone thoughts come to mind
In wondering what a mess, lives lost
Countries suffering, children needing attention
A decent living, food, water, the necessities of life
Forgotten. Small considerations, millions stupidly spent
To no avail. Ignorance seems to be the benchmark of life
Four years wasted. Do you suppose our nation will survive?

PAT & ED

Patti Ann and Ed Goganti
Niece and nephew of mine
Having not seen them for awhile
But frequently come to mind.
They used to come and visit
With parents Bernice and Joe
When we lived on Edwards Street
That was many years ago.

Now executive Ed lives in St. Louis
Pat a pharmacist at Walgreens
If you need scripts filled
How about a visit
Trying to keep in touch
With nieces and nephews
Through years of time
I feel their guardian angel
Watch over them
Along with prayers of mine.

WHILE

There is a word in each dictionary
Seen to boggle my mind
Out of the ordinary
The other day
I ask someone
Are you busy
I will help you
After <u>while.</u>

A thought that made me dizzy
Who is this "<u>while</u>"
I wondered what were they doing then
Was <u>while</u> time
A minute
Did I offend
I'm not really excited
What was *after* doing
I just said forget I asked
It's not worth pursuing.

WORDS FROM A WORD

Many years ago
Teacher Agnes Longerman
Trying to keep students busy
During a terrible storm
She devised a plan saying
Everyone get your tablet
Write the word "teacher"
Now find words of
Three or more letters of the alphabet
You can make starting with "T"
Then "e", "a", "c" and so on.

Tar-tare-tea-teak-tree-three-trace-thee-there-the
Eat-ear-erect-era-each
Ace-act-ache-ate-are-and
cat-care-cart-chat-crate-cheer-create-char
Hat-hate-hare-here-hear-heat-her
e-double letter
Rat-rate-race-react-reach.

The teacher offered prizes for those who found 20 or more. No dictionary was allowed. I won't forget my number, The entire class received an apple. Storm over, everyone went home happy. So many little simple things back then brought fun and enriched our lives.

WHOLE — HOLE

Listen very carefully
Someone saying
I ate the *whole* thing.

Was it something you dug
Or a sock that needed darning
A *hole* is what
You dig to plant a tree
Two things are a fact
Eating a *whole* pie or cake
In a *hole* well
You could fall flat.

AFTER

When hearing or using the word <u>after,</u> what can it mean?

AFTER

ALL—ENTIRE GROUP
EACH ONE—INDIVIDUAL
TOMORROW—NEVER COMES
YESTERDAY—DAY PASSED
TODAY—WHAT NEXT
A WHILE—SOONER OR LATER
SCHOOL—NO BOOKS
SPEAKING—QUIET
YOU LEFT—BYE-BYE
A TALK—GAB FEST
WHAT YOU DID—GOOD OR BAD
BEING HERE—STAY AWAY
SUNRISE—START WORKING
THE PARTY OVER—GO HOME
HELPING YOU—SO WHAT
NOON—ONE O'CLOCK
ALL IS WELL—WERE YOU ILL

WANDERING

With family, friends living around the U.S. and aboard, a travel log comes to mind. Leaving Ormond Beach, first stop to see John Sorman in Auburndale, then Peg Scott and family in Lakeland. Then up I-75 to Atlanta to visit Marilyn Walsh Bunn. On to Texas, visit granddaughter Tricia Cross in Houston; a short distance to see niece Ruth Ann Masters and husband Ken in Conroe. Catch a flight into St. Louis, visit Lynette & Jim Poschel, nephew Ed Giganti. On to Belleville (IL) visit nephew Tom Edwards, wife Alexa, son Andrew and daughter Morgan. Up to Jacksonville to visit Lori, Brent, Jacob & Josh Padhe. Travel east with a stop in New Berlin to see Sharon and Mark Price, on to Chatham to see Bob & Peg Vander-Heiden, Steve & Marilyn Markus, Rena Valorez, Lucille Gibson, Barbara and Dwight Morrison, Mike and Sharon Crowley Also a visit to St. Joseph's Church and the Chatham Cemetery. Next stop Springfield, plan to see Kathleen, Barbara, Gregory and Don Edwards, Sister Pauletta Overbeck, Don Bacon, Maurice "*Dewey*" "Dewimille, Harlan McTaggart, Patti Giganti, Joe and Mary Fitz, Mick & Fran Ryan, Don & Cinda Kincade. Theresa & Ernie Grieme, the Dominican Sisters Pauletta & Francis Mary, Howard & Shirley Reynolds and Mike Evans. It would be nice to also visit the new Abraham Lincoln Pressidental Library and just see all the changes to the downtown scape in the last ten years. Then out to Ashland for some time with Dolores (Sis) Edwards and Jim, Rich & Shirley; nephew Ed (wife Mary) Orne, niece Helen Orne Strubbe and her family. Continuing east to Decatur to see Charlie and Charlotte Munie. North to Wisconsin to see niece Caroline Stelte Kysley and family, then Mary Crowley Harman and family in Michigan. Heading back south, stop in Galena to see Maureen Edwards Fletcher and Greg, then to Palatine for a reunion with Dick and Betty Kunzweiler, daugther Diane and sons Steve, Dave, Kent, Kevin and their families, and nearby Joe Burlini, Eleanor Sheehy and Brother Leo Ryan in Arlington Heights, and before boarding the flight to Las Vegas to see Niece Shirley Scott Traver, at least a phone call to Raoul Allesee. From O'Hare International, on to San Diego to meet Terry & Missy Edwards. Next a hope to Hawaii to see Jerry Bristow at his home in Honolulu. The journey now takes several long flights. Navan, Ireland to see Sr. Paula Brennan, Celle Germany to see Maggie, Ingrid, Helmet, Rolf, Birgit, Sascha, and Timo Kremeike, on to Perth Australia to visit Jack, Carole, Kristine, Richard, & Stephanie Clarke and finally Dubai in the UAE to spent some time with Izzit, Stacey, Nathaniel, Zachary and Benjamin Guney. Each of these families living abroad have visited my Ormond Beach again. When they are able to again come to the states, my welcome mat and red carpet is ready to rollout.

THE GYPSY IN ME

The places I've traveled: Europe
England, Ireland, Scotland, Wales, Italy, Switzerland, Budapest, Prague, Belgrade,
Venice, Vienna
And the Eastern and Western Caribbean,
San Juan and the provinces of Canada
And most of our beloved United States
God Bless America

Just a wanderer, that is me
There is a lot of world to see
No matter where you travel
Summer, winter, spring or fall
Let your anxieties unravel
Much better than a trip to the mall

ARIZONA STEPS

These steps a miracle
The higher you climb
A great accomplishment
When reaching a platform sign
Climbing steps a fantasy
How many times daily taken
Realize when evening comes
You were not mistaken
Many of mine traveling
Taos, Las Vegas, California, New York
Statue of Liberty visited
Mastermind creator took
What a trip to Arizona
Walk across 4,000' high bridge
I would not be afraid
View surrounding areas
Worth the effort made
Great credit to builders
Hoping to create
Many dollars for charity
Regardless of the rate
Bridge builders everywhere
Spread knowledge from others
Happiness to tribes Arizona way
Money for educating children
Brothers, sisters, fathers, mothers.

HE CARES

For all nations
May God bless each day you awake
Trouble in war zones
Getting difficult to take.
Many our Americans
Suffering, neglected care
Reading about injuries
Agony, despair.
Recently father O'Malley
Sent item to read
From a priest friend
Coming home from Germany
Shedding tears brought to mind
What a waste of humanity.
Those who caused problems
For the USA and beyond
Where is the end
Dear God our savior
Hear our prayers
On you we depend.

7 MAY 2007

Here we are another date
Fires burning in our Florida state
No thunder, lightning
Cause for debate
A casual match, cigarette, bonfire
Simple carelessness.
Problems firemen working overtime
Find no answer yet
Who, what can we fault. Please understand
See the ashes extinguished
Before leaving your hand.

NO

You ask, were you singing
When I passed by
My answer no
Thank you
Twas a Monarch butterfly.

DID YOU EVER WONDER

Seasons run spring to winter
Warmer weather in summer
Fall leaves start shedding
Winter snowflakes glitter
Cold temperature dreading.
I like roses blooming
Rain drops in the air
Falling on the thirsty earth
Beautiful lawns everywhere
Suddenly no sun shining
Thunder, lightning a storm
Abounds in danger
Even birds cannot be found.
Then wonder why trees are different
Traveling from state to state
We enjoy pecans and peaches
From Georgia really great
Windmills in California
Few seen elsewhere
Most other states grow veggies
Used around the world
Corn Illinois, Iowa, Kansas wheat
Idaho potatoes, Florida cabbage
When traveling give them all a whirl
Forget not those producing petrol
All cars use gas and oil.

ST. PAUL'S

There is a church in Daytona Beach Florida
Called the Basilica of St. Paul
A magnificent structure, elegant, beautiful
To visit, enjoy, pray.
Father Tim Daly the pastor
Sent recently to serve
Folks from all walks of life
School children receive care
One thing a choir of note
Voices none can compare
David McGhee, organ also piano
Manuel a baritone rare
Great when singing solo
Like a day in spring.
The choir tours include
Travel through Italy and Ireland
Singing at the Vatican
For the pope's audience and Sunday Mass
Each member doing a full share
At midnight Mass I attended
Church filled to overflowing
Then in 2006 Fr. Bob Webster leaving
After serving many years with care
His Mass and the choir
Singing, music extraordinaire.

CHANCE

A chance to give
A chance to laugh
A chance to sign my autograph.
A chance worthwhile
To sing a song
A chance to feel you belong
A chance of doing
What you please
A chance of seeing
Kites flying in the breeze.

HURRY—SLOW-TIME

Why do people say "hurry up"
I want to shout
What is hurry doing
Does he have a name
I would like to hear about?

When someone says "slow down"
Was he going too fast
These are words often heard
Might have good meanings
That will not last.

Some say "take your time"
Where do you take it
Time is of the essence
My thoughts are "shake it".

Put hurry—slow—time
Store away together
Give me sunshine each day I live
Keep me safe no matter the weather.

TO — FOR

To awaken each morning
Tonight someone alert
Tomorrow send greetings
To never cause hurt
To offer congratulations
For a happy birthday
To share a luncheon
To brighten their day
To walk in their footsteps
To make each worthwhile
To understand feelings
To hug when they cry
To hear children laughing
To teach them right from wrong
To show encouragement
To help each grow strong
For reaching helping hands
For remembering tomorrow
For making no demands
To aid someone in sorrow
For happiness always
To hold someone tight
For life so precious
To all a goodnight.

ALPHABETICAL—HMMM

A—advantage—use

B beguile—amuse

C contentment—sigh

D distribute—buy

E exile—deceive

F fantastic—believe

G genuine—read

H hereafter—appeal

I ignore—unkind

J jeopardy—find

K keeping—score

L learning—more

M minority—win

N neglect—sin

O opinion—alert

P protect—not hurt

Q quality—perfect

R restore—worth

S sympathy—sad

T temptation—bad

U useless—not me

V vanity—agree

W wasteful—save

X x-ray—brave

Y youngster—hello

Z zero—cold below

TAX

Need time doing things
Take a break relax
Especially reviewing
Your income tax.

HAY

Ring around the hay stack
This I must say
Stay away from that skunk
Hiding in the bale of hay

QUESTIONS

Ask no questions
Tell no lies
Closing your mouth
You won't catch flies.

ABUSE

Never let
Your tongue run loose
Wrong remarks
Cause abuse.

YARD

A yard to mow, a yard to buy
To make a dress
Don't make a mess

03-24-07

At dawn skies were cloudy
Soon parting with delight
Sun appeared like magic
Blue sky showing a majestic sight.

The change on earth we enjoy
Must create a vision
Gives all the chance
Making a decision.

Say a prayer for men
Wearing a uniform
Soon may they return
To homelands where born.

Many of our family
Served in War One
About 300 cousins served
Wore many different uniforms.

So I welcome day of life
And pray for those who sacrificed

LIFE

Each life given we implore
Grant many in this world that gave their life
Were given heaven's golden door.
Many on earth believe
They're doing something great
What does our future hold
Problems happening in every state.
Many tears of loneliness
Appear in our universe
Little children suffering
Needing protection, health and food
Love of life from bad to worse
Not doing much at 92
Still hoping time will create
Peace before it is too late
How much must we endure.

LOOK

Look up
Look down
Look around
Look ahead
Look about
A child playing baseball
Stand up and shout
Look forward
Look back
Look at the ocean
Look at the sand
Look at rain falling
To moisten the land
Look at the moon
Look at the stars
Look at fireflies
Look at clouds
High in the sky
Look back at yesterday
Look for tomorrow
Look where times goes
Hour by hour.

TO DAVID

Life
Something to live
Something to learn
Something to give
Happiness impart
Believing, share
Your talent rare.

Your letter the answer
To fantastic living.
You find enjoyment
When the organ you play
For me listening pleasure
Especially Sunday

I keep my fingers busy
Writing prose and poetry
Just as you David
Beautify the do, re, mi
Always so lovingly.

Your thoughtful expression
Wonderful to read
Keep feet, thumbs, fingers nimble
Continue to exceed.

STATES AND THEIR CAPITALS

And some musings

Alabama—Montgomery
Cotton grown here makes you kerchoo

Alaska—Juneau
Ice flows, snow to view

Arkansas—Little Rock
Tobacco, chickens raised

Arizona—Phoenix
Herds of cattle graze

California—Sacramento
Beautiful golden west

Colorado—Denver
Mountain skiing best

Connecticut—Hartford
Great to see

Delaware—Dover
Name alone will please

Florida—Tallahassee
College here Florida State

Georgia—Atlanta
Peaches, pecans great

Hawaii—Honolulu
Surfing really grand

Idaho—Boise
Potatoes here in demand

Illinois—Springfield
Lincoln's home town land

Indiana—Indianapolis
Famous memorial Day race

Iowa—Des Moines
Corn here every place

Kansas—Topeka
I attended convention here

Kentucky—Frankfort
Horse farms to cheer

Louisiana—Baton Rouge
Folks here play piano

Maine—Augusta
Lobster not a no-no

Maryland—Annapolis
A happy sounding name

Massachusetts—Boston
Tea Party named here

Michigan—Lansing
Great state any time of year

Minnesota—St. Paul
Minneapolis close to view

Missouri—Jefferson City
State where born "Howdy-do"

Mississippi—Jackson
Spell it Backwards for fun

Montana—Helena
Land of a rising sun

Nebraska—Lincoln
Carries a president's name

Nevada—Carson City
Slot machines, costly game

New Hampshire—Concord
On the eastern seaboard

New Jersey—Trenton
Not to be ignored

New Mexico—Santa Fe
People here love to celebrate

New York—Albany
The big apple state

Ohio—Columbus
Carries Christopher's name

Oklahoma—Oklahoma City
State with its own song

Oregon—Salem
May visit before long

Pennsylvania—Harrisburg
Visit here, don't hesitate

Rhode Island—Providence
The smallest eastern state

North Dakota—Bismarck
You find many deer

South Dakota—Pierre
At memorial time visit here

North Carolina—Raleigh
Capital Known for someone great
South Carolina—Columbia
Kept clean and up to date

Tennessee—Nashville
Grand ol' opry famous here

Texas—Austin
Largest state give a cheer

Utah—Salt Lake City
Mormon Tabernacle choir grand

Vermont—Montpelier
Cabot cheese made here in demand

Virginia—Richmond
Here they play the xzylophone

Washington—Olympia
Where "Peace on earth" should be known

West Virginia—Charleston
People here love to tease

Wisconsin—Madison
Where you find delicious cheese

Wyoming—Cheyenne
Last in line if you please.

When you need a game to play
Naming state capitals makes a fun day.

SCHOOL

Seeing a child happy
Ease his pain when sad
Offering of any kind
Both will enjoy
The best day ever had.

EARTH

A dusty road was traveled
Seeing farmers plowing the earth
Ready for planting corn wheat oats
Wondering are my efforts worth
When planted will we soon have rain
So the seed will sprout
Moisture needed appreciated
Then farmers give a shout
Come on guys let's get prepared
Each doing his share
A successful harvest given tender care.

PEAK

I climbed the peak of contentment
Not far from good mother earth
Each step I took
Really no words because
I was there on the day of my birth.

MEASURE

When cooking for excitement
Start while living at home
Each day find pleasure
A yard you will measure
Like giving your dog a bone.

TIME

Each day pursuing a good time
Do something for someone living alone.

TRAVELING THE BYWAYS

A million miles or more
Traveling on airplanes
Reaching many foreign shores
Traveling on seas and oceans
To counties and island everywhere
Traveling in autos
Through many of our states
Trains like magic
This I know
Serve food that is great
Horse and buggy
Busses, taxis everywhere
When visiting a town or city
Be sure you take a camera
Capture scenes mighty pretty
So what if this travel takes a year
You will store memories dear.

IF I

If I counted the times
Having said, I love you
They would reach a mile
Am I foolish to believe
You do the same with a smile.

A RULE

Looking back on yesterday
Without a regret
Wondering if along the way
Did I almost forget
Share a smile, say hello
Gently clasp a hand
Never be self-centered
A rule I must not bend.
Everyone has known or felt
Aches pain and sorrow
In remembering yesterdays
Let's spread more joy tomorrow.
A flower blooms, then fades away
The leaves fall from trees
Your creation all of things
Gives joy that will never cease.
Life is good in all ways
Faith has been a treasure
Thanks I give each day I live
Happiness long on measure.

JOE, OUR SECRET

Tears in my eyes darling
Pain won't go away
Loving one of the good things
Sure as night turns into day.

May you enjoy the very best
Blessings come your way
I'll not forget the thoughts we shared
Each time I kneel to pray.

You will ever walk beside me
Keeping you close will be a part
The way that I have loved you
Our secret from the start.

Not ashamed, it was precious
Gave me pleasures never known
Something to forever cherish
That belongs to me alone.

HE KNOWS

I keep praying you will call
Come see me again
Giving help whenever I could
Wishing you no pain.
We have faults, this God knows
Without him where would we be
If loving you I lost again
I'm lucky prayers are free.

THE TEST

Why doubt the outcome of your life
You believe in God
His power is the greatest
Help given as we trod.

Be kind to all around you
Bring happy days to friends
Thankful for the small things
Much on this depends.

We know giving the best way
Sharing puts us to the test
Our life is filled with doing
Adds a little zest.

Thinking that tomorrow
The most precious day we live
If hurt we have a chance
Ask, will you forgive?

HONOR

Being alone for quite awhile
I thought love passed me by
Then you came into my life
   Now hopes are high.

Please dearest never go away
Leaving would bring sorrow
I promise to love and honor
Each dawning of tomorrow.

HELLO

What better may begin your day
With a friendly greeting
Someone you see along the way
Make a worthwhile meeting.
How are you, a question everyone asks
It could mean so much
Remember loneliness ceases
Whenever we keep in touch.
Good morning, hello, so special
Really not hard to say
When kind to a friend
Before days end
Good things come your way.
A ray of sunshine
Blotted out the darkness
A smile ended the lonesome feeling
A laugh eased the agony
When you whispered
Hello, believe me.

WORDS

Words by the dozens
Plentiful as cousins
With so many it's hard keeping track
I love them dearly
Though tell you sincerely
Words don't ever talk back.

NO FROWN

Did you ever think that loneliness
Was picking just on you
Others have their problems
Troubles, especially when blue.

Never place your burden
On anyone you meet
Just scattered a little sunshine
Life will seem more sweet.

Make the most of everyday
Doing this you find
Smiling is a pleasure
A frown not worth a dime.

Pleasures come from giving
Think, may I advise
Someone not so fortunate
With sadness in their eyes.

Don't feel sorry for yourself
Think happy, have more fun
Sacrifice twice as nice
Enjoy living, it's just begun.

TRUE

Sadness and sorrow
Are for tomorrow
Believe this everyday
Because tomorrow never comes
Each could be a happy day.

EACH HOUR

Follow the nomad on his journey
Seeking the rainbow trail
Gaze at the swallow soaring above
Enjoy breeze like the wind blown sail.

Then will your heart beat faster
When seeing a friendly smile
Keep you from growing weary
Making the hours worthwhile.

Follow the man on a flying trapeze
View magic of planes flying high
Look at the beautiful shining sun
At night see stars in the sky.

Keep loved ones hopes alive
Willingly answer their call.
Try to achieve, trust and believe
The Master takes care of all.

ILLINOIS NEIGHBORS

Listing of the names below
Mean so much you'll see
While reading off the line-up
Share a smile with me.

Gibson, Vallorz, Cudworth, Crouch
Koenig, Crowley, Lynn, Scott, Creasy
Kingery, Marcus, VanderHeiden, Kunzweiler
Spelling some names not so easy.

The young folks are growing
Beautiful you should see
If all places were like Crestview Drive
How great living would be.

We have Linda G.
Ernest, Alert and Lynda V.
Jake, Nancy, Larry, Mary, Jim and Kate
Kevin, Tracy, Ric, Connie, Ken and Kaye
And Colleen Markus who moved up state.

Stacy V. lives next door to me
Her catTigger is our friend
My son Don the last on the list
Here my poems must end.

978-0-595-46780-8
0-595-46780-6

Printed in the United States
96380LV00003B/46-69/A